THIS IS SOCIAL COMMERCE

THIS IS SOCIAL COMMERCE

Turning Social Media into Sales

Guy Clapperton

CAPSTONE

This edition first published 2012
© 2012 Guy Clapperton

Registered office
John Wiley & Sons Ltd, The Atrium, Southern Gate, Chichester, West Sussex, PO19 8SQ, United Kingdom

For details of our global editorial offices, for customer services and for information about how to apply for permission to reuse the copyright material in this book please see our website at www.wiley.com.

Library of Congress Cataloging-in-Publication Data

Clapperton, Guy.
    This is social commerce : turning social media into sales / Guy Clapperton.
      p. cm.
    Includes bibliographical references and index.
    ISBN 978-0-857-08241-1 (pbk.)
    1. Electronic commerce—Social aspects.   2. Internet marketing—Social aspects.   3. Cooperative societies.
4. Consumer cooperatives.   5. Online social networks.   6. Social media.   I. Title.
    HF5548.32.C53   2012
    658.8'72—dc23

                                                                                    2011044312

A catalogue record for this book is available from the British Library.

ISBN 978-0-857-08241-1 (paperback) ISBN 978-0-857-08253-4 (ebk)
ISBN 978-0-857-08254-1 (ebk)   ISBN 978-0-857-08255-8 (ebk)

Set in 10/15pt Akkurat Light by Toppan Best-set Premedia Limited, Hong Kong
Printed in Great Britain by TJ International Ltd, Padstow, Cornwall, UK

CONTENTS

INTRODUCTION: THE DEATH OF ATTENTION

It's early winter and I've been invited to give a keynote speech to a conference. It's about social media and whether it's really making money for people or not, and whether it's performing as a business tool. As I try to find the venue, someone I've never met points me in the right direction.

They've recognized me from my picture on Twitter, which is flattering. I wonder, perhaps idly, how many other people half-recognize people from their Twitter streams these days – it's a network that encourages communication with strangers after all.

I get to the venue and make my introductions. My turn to speak arrives and I look out at the audience. Many are looking at me but an equal number are looking down at laptops, at a phone in their hands. I try to get their attention, joking, being serious, but nothing appears to be working. It's only after the conference that I see why, when I'm on the train home. I check my Twitter stream on my phone and find that it's packed with mentions of me.

They don't all agree with what I was saying by any means, which suits me fine – anyone can do a presentation that scratches people's egos. But all these people, the ones who had their heads down, were actually discussing the content of my presentation, for and against, with people who either were or weren't there.

I start my next presentation another time with 'Hello, the top of everybody's heads.' Nobody gets it – they really don't know they're doing it. A few months later I attend a meeting of the Professional Speaking Association and one of the speakers asks people not to do this. If you're in the room, please be present in the room, he says.

I don't think I'd have the guts to do that. And anyway I'm more interested in the psychology of what's happening to the people in the audience. OK, they're younger than me, I admit it – but something about their attitude has changed. Here's a diagram of how speaking has worked until now:

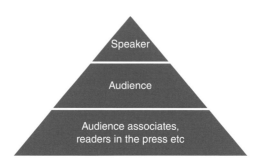

The speaker speaks first, then within a split second the audience hears and ingests what he or she has said. It's only much later that the audience starts spreading the word – if you're lucky. A timeline might run:

- 2pm: Speaker presents at a breakout session. Audience assimilates immediately.

- 2.30pm: Session breaks up, audience starts chatting, information still largely confined to audience.

- 3pm: Coffee break, information might start spreading around primarily among people attending the conference

- 6pm: Social time – content *starts* disseminating around people who weren't there – colleagues, friends.

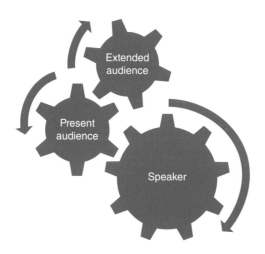

This diagram can now be changed for a more modern audience thus:

The speaker is presenting to two audiences, one he or she can see and one he or she can't. The invisible audience is feeding back to the audience in the room and they'll be feeding back to the speaker too, assuming there's a decent question and answer session. Some presenters might even have a live feed of comments running on a screen in the background so that they can interact with their absentee audience on the spot. It's worth keeping an eye on these though – there's always some joker who wants to get a cheap laugh by making a rude comment about the speaker! The new timeline looks something like this:

- 3pm: Speaker starts presentation.

- 3.01: Tweeting and Facebook commentaries start about the content and the style.

- 3.01 and a bit: People in different continents start seeing content and commenting on it.

This is how the new audience is starting to behave. You can call them generation Y if you like and a lot of marketers do, but it's not so much an age-based generation as a technology and communications affair. It's not just kids doing this – people in their forties, fifties, and beyond are Tweeting, updating their Facebook entries, and bringing interactions into real time.

The new demographic

The audience is changing and it's changing because of what we now categorize as social media. That much isn't in any doubt; just how they're changing and what their expectations are needs to be understood by anyone who wants to sell to them. And in spite of the noise that's been made about sharing everything and how selfless the social media and its advocates are, selling is still an important concept.

A couple of years ago, News International decided to put *The Times* newspaper behind a paywall. If you wanted to see more than today's paper and you weren't a registered subscriber, you had to pay. Meanwhile, there were huge amounts of freebies around the place. Companies like Google were giving away office software in their Google Docs suite, while Facebook and Twitter were giving away free social networking applications.

In the presentation mentioned earlier, I asked whether people were using any of these and basing their business planning on the fact that they didn't have to pay. A number confirmed that they were using Google Docs as their only office tools. They didn't see any problem in this, since they were marketing themselves through Facebook and Twitter as well.

However, my point to them, and to you, is that this won't be sustainable forever. It needs to be paid for by someone, and the person using the service is the most likely candidate. At some point, the businesses behind these applications will have to make their transactions about money rather than continue to give them away. Social networking-based businesses need to be realistic and so do their customers; if a company isn't making money it will eventually have to drop a service, and if your business is dependent on that service you'll need a 'plan B' in case that service ever stops. Expecting it all for nothing in perpetuity is not reasonable.

When making these suggestions at the presentation, the reactions on Twitter and Face-book were sharply divided. A vocal minority felt I was talking sense and that this needed to be said even louder. More people chimed in with disagreements – either respectfully or with comments like 'Guy Clapperton just doesn't get it, does he?' One participant said they hadn't expected me to speak in favour of News International, and in the post hacking scandal world, that looks a lot more of an obvious point than it did at the time. As one person put it: 'We *do* pay, with our contact details and with our friends.'

This is an interesting comment and a view I'd heard before. People honestly feel that they are 'paying' for things by offering their friends' details. Do these friends know they're being used as hard currency? It seems to suggest a new means of conducting business online. That the relationship moves from a straight customer-pays-supplier route to something a little more like this:

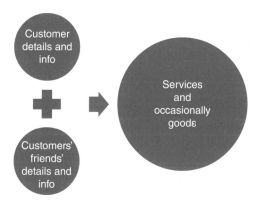

I'm actually pretty suspicious of an equation that looks as though it's built like that. My main problem is that nowhere does money or anything like it appear. Some people see it as a sort of virtuous circle in which we all end up living by some sort of means of exchange of intellectual property. What I say is, show me how it makes money or I won't believe it's sustainable. Adopting it to the exclusion of all other business models appears to me to be risky in the extreme.

My belief – and I suspect the belief of a lot of people buying this book – was, and is, that businesses either supplying or using the social networks need to understand exactly how they will end up paying for themselves. My first book on the subject, *This is Social Media*, makes a lot out of putting a business plan in place for any social media engagements and ensuring they have a target and an objective. I was surprised at the vehemence with which some people disagreed.

Within a few months of that conference taking place I felt pretty vindicated. The social bookmarking service, Delicious, was going to be sold off or scrapped by its then owner Yahoo! The reason, just as I'd predicted, was that it wasn't making money. It was a free facility over the Internet, offering people the chance to bookmark their favourite websites either privately with a password or publicly to share on their website or on the social networks.

Yahoo! simply couldn't see a financial justification for continuing the service. It wasn't bringing money in and unless someone was missing something fairly substantial it stood no chance of doing so. It managed to sell the service rather than close it but it was clear that a very substantial owner indeed had no interest in continuing with it.

My point is that in spite of the apparent beliefs of some people, the underlying pattern of business and how it happens hasn't changed. You offer goods or a service and if you find it's not paying then one of these days you're going to withdraw it.

Mobile social

Back to my presentation that day. Afterwards I nip into a bookshop intending to buy a book, or magazine, or something. As I pick up a current paperback to browse through, I glance at the man next to me.

He's fiddling with his mobile phone.

Nothing uncommon in that, you're thinking, people fiddle with their phones all the time and everywhere. But he's fiddling with it in the middle of a book shop and *he is looking at the Amazon mobile site.*

Look, I understand people shopping around. I have often gone from one January Sale to another, picking among the bargains to find the better price. But I've never quite had the brass neck to stand on someone else's premises and check the price whilst holding the book in my hand.

He may not have been checking prices, of course. He may have had the Kindle app on his phone, and decided to download the book on the spot.

Maybe he wasn't doing that at all. Maybe he was just finding out whether the book was any good – nobody in the shop was about to tell him. Perhaps he had intended to buy a physical copy for the train but wasn't sure whether he'd like it or not. So instead of reading the cover, leafing through and taking a chance, he looked at Amazon to see how the book was rated and how many people had bothered to review it.

You might call this 'social buying.' People check their purchases not just with friends but with complete strangers before making them. It's an odd thing until you consider that every review on the back of a book's jacket is going to be positive – maybe even selectively quoted. Amazon's readers will be less fettered.

So will TripAdvisor's readers if you're going on holiday. So will TopTable's reviewers if you're looking for a restaurant, and so on. Customers, particularly large numbers of customers, are starting – consciously or otherwise – to mobilize themselves. The business that's aware is going to do well out of it; the one that isn't will find things tougher.

This change towards peer advice through social media is causing actual psychology to change, I'm convinced. I check my Twitter feed and I find a load of people telling me where they are, and telling me their comments on their whereabouts through the new social network called FourSquare. Some of them have become mayors.

Well, no they haven't – just in FourSquare's eyes. But they're stars in their own eyes and they've become such by announcing where they are to whoever happens to be following them on Twitter.

A colleague was interested in this so she asked a few young people why they felt compelled to announce where they were the whole time through their social media stream. She was met with shrugs and 'because it's social' and the inference that of *course* they told people where they were, all their friends did it and you didn't want to be left out. It was natural to them – a bit like someone of my generation trying to explain why watching entertainment on the television was a normal thing to do if a listener had never seen it.

Social buyers can of course get discounts if they turn up at a FourSquare establishment – or a Facebook Place, or get Groupon tokens. This seems not to be the main reason for the behaviour, though – people's attitudes to a lot of things are changing. People saying they pay for services with friends' details, people who see no inconsistency between any notion of privacy and announcing exactly where they are at any particular time – these are new behaviours.

What this book isn't

All that's been said so far is the backdrop. That's the new attitude and some of the new expectations against which this book is being written. For all that, though, I'm not here to explain how the new businesses are going to make money using the new financial models and I'm not here to be a middle-aged author going on about how young people always think they can re-invent the universe.

There are people making money in this new scenario and I applaud them. Facebook, for example, has made loads of money in advertising and as a result it's comfortably in profit and has been for a while – it keeps getting valued for huge amounts by Wall Street and its investors.

I'm not assuming you will become the new Facebook by reading this book. This isn't a book on how to make a killing in what, for all we know, is another dotcom boom set to come crashing down just like the last one.

This isn't a psychology book, although I'm sure there's an interesting one to be written about how this new generation thinks. I'm not qualified to write about it in depth.

What this book is

This is a book for people who want their business to adapt to the new digital generation without assuming that all commercial reality has changed – I don't believe it has. This is the way to cope with this new digitally-aware customer and in particular the commerce they transact. They make groups, they consider the Internet a human right (don't look at me like that, the European Union agrees), and they expect to behave as a group. This is how to take advantage of the herd mentality when you can be part of the same electronic club that's bringing the herd together.

I've aimed for a book which is practical rather than theoretical. You'll find many case studies and interviews with people in business who've done this stuff in real life, and who are happy to talk about their success, where they've fallen short, and – let's be realistic – where they've run out of time. This is business. This is reality. This is social commerce.

1 WELCOME TO SOCIAL COMMERCE

Social commerce,' like the subject often associated with it, social media, isn't brand new but it's being done in a brand new way. This chapter should help explain the concept and ensure you're able to establish whether it will help your business at all. Businesses and customers are changing and the aim of this and every other part of this book is to help you adapt to those changes.

You should also walk away from this chapter with a number of ideas of how to build a following and work out how this can actually help you build up a business.

So what, precisely, do I mean when I talk about social commerce? Many sorts of commerce can be described as 'social' and you have to zero in on it a little before it starts to become really meaningful.

Let me explain this with a scenario. Say you want to buy something simple like a pack of butter. How would you describe the process? You go out, get a plot of land, seed it, grow grass, feed a cow, milk the cow, churn the milk, and then scrape the butter off the sides and put it in a packet. Is that right?

No it's not and you know it. It's rubbish. But it's what happens when you go and buy a pack of butter. Somewhere along the line all of that stuff has happened, or something vaguely like it – anyone reading this who's in agriculture is by now probably killing themselves laughing at my oversimplification. Nonetheless the problem you'd face if you tried to buy everything just for yourself is that it's impossible to make any economies when you're just making one-offs.

So you get a bit social. A group of you go to a trader and suggest you want butter. The trader goes to a farmer and says, I can introduce you to this number of people to sell your butter, but you've got to bring the price down. The farmer says he or she would be delighted – and that is people being social to make commerce happen. So in order to buy anything at all for what might be thought a reasonable price, you have to be social in some respect otherwise it simply can't add up. This, at its most basic, is social commerce.

We're going to have to be a bit more specific than that, obviously. Otherwise everyone will think it's easy.

Defining social commerce

Truer forms of social commerce might be said to have started with the co-operative movement, which survives to the present day not only in the form of the Co-Op but also in experiments like the 'People's Supermarket' movement. The idea here is that a group of individuals get together to bypass the big corporate money-making conglomerates and source their food collectively. They bypass the traditional suppliers and go to smaller producers, the tiny growers on allotments, the farms who'll deal direct, and they set their own prices. Instead of profit they plough money back in and award themselves dividends, or extra discounts – non-members are welcome to buy but the price will be slightly higher.

This is a little more to do with what I'm going to describe as the modern version of social commerce. It's not the whole thing, though, and there are parts of the revived model which aren't wholly relevant. For example, this book isn't going to be unduly concerned with idealistic principles on whether big or small business should or should not make a profit. We'll be talking about people like Facebook, Google, and Groupon. These are substantial companies which either have been listed or are heading for it. They have been valued at billions and are doing very nicely out of social commerce, thanks.

This book will take as its thesis that social commerce is commerce made possible when a large group of suppliers meets a large group of buyers, and they haggle as groups and achieve the best possible price. The medium through which this happens is the Internet, just because it's the easiest way of getting so many people together.

That's not all this book is going to be about. That's the most pure form of 'social commerce' by all means but there's another facet, an overlay that seems to have invited itself along during the 21st century. That was the subject of my previous book, *This is Social Media*. Social media or social networking (the terms are interchangeable) allows the customer to communicate directly with the producer and to have a conversation. The producer gets to know the customer and can detect trends – among the more voluble customers anyway. The producer can publicize, cajole people into taking part and buying, float ideas, research the likely responses.

As I said in the Introduction, a lot of this is happening because the customer has changed and is now digitally aware. There are lots of clichés around about how people have become empowered, how the customer is king, how engagement is everything. These are mostly clichés because they're right. The Internet means the customer has more options to switch suppliers half way through a transaction than ever before. This puts them in the driving seat more than ever before.

This chapter will focus on how the social customer is taking advantage of the sort of deal that has only become possible because mass buying is in place, and how the technology has been harnessed to make deals happen.

An early social business: Naked Wines

Overall the aim of a social commerce-oriented business is to make the customer feel part of the company even when they're not technically a shareholder. This is something at which Naked Wines has been very good indeed. There is much to be gained from observing how the business makes people feel they are part of something, so the rest of this chapter will take this example in some depth.

Naked Wines is a wine club based in the UK – Norwich to be specific. It operates completely online; there are no shop fronts, no wine warehouses to visit. It is a classic example of the electronic medium introducing buyers and sellers.

There were attempts at making this happen much earlier; you might recall companies like Letsbuyit.com, which had the idea of bringing together small business customers, getting them to act en bloc and buying printers, computers, and so forth at good prices. The pitch to the seller was that these people were effectively acting like a much larger enterprise.

The reason for the failure at that stage, and we're talking late 1990s here, was that people took impossible positions. Suppliers offered thousands of small businesses tiny discounts, less than they'd typically get from a decent dealer. The businesses, meanwhile, all wanted a top of the range laser printer for a tenner. The positions taken were ridiculous so the idea fell to pieces.

Naked Wines and other modern counterparts prefer to be more realistic, and focus on the achievable. If you want to join Naked Wines and just buy wine cases that's fine. Nobody's going to mind, you just go ahead. To get more out of it, though, you become a 'wine angel.' This involves sending the organization twenty quid a month. It then puts this into an account for you and you can buy wine with it or have it back if you change your mind – there's no catch.

It then goes to small wine producers, who don't get into the supermarkets or bigger wine clubs, and puts a proposition to them. That proposition is: Naked Wines can offer them cash flow because of the regular payments from 'angels,' as long as the wine makers in question offer a preferential price to the customers in question.

The existing model

The Internet has allowed the gathering together of buyers and sellers to adopt terms and conditions they find mutually beneficial, says founder Rowan Gormley. If individuals were to try to get together and make this sort of deal happen it simply wouldn't work.

There is an argument that says the financial model on which most of the Western World is based has become flawed because of too many intermediaries. The buyer and seller have so many people between them who need to be paid. The buyer spends money on having products marketed to them, on having products marketed to the wholesaler, on shipments to intermediary points and on a great deal else before their money goes near the actual price of the product. 'The consumer is getting poor value and the (product) supplier is struggling to make a living and it's just because of the inefficiency of the way commerce is involved,' says Gormley. And so the Internet became the mechanism by which companies like Naked Wines are able to get things moving and repair this apparent problem.

It's not just a matter of saying 'we're on the Internet so please send us regular money,' though. Gormley explains it using his co-founder Francesca Krajewski as an example. 'Let's say I introduce Fran as a wine maker and ask if you'd like to give her a hundred quid – you'd say you needed to know more. But if we say to people, "give us twenty quid a month and we'll sort out immediate delivery and all the boring bits", we get a response.'

So far so old media – but in this case the social element adds a great deal to the transactions taking place. To stick with the example on the table, Fran doesn't just ask for money. She introduces herself as a wine maker, tells you about herself, joins a social network, explains the wines on which she is working and why she thinks they'll be any good. She answers questions, listens to feedback, and the end results feature in her product. People who want to get more involved in the wines they buy have that opportunity.

Obviously this isn't going to matter to everyone – many people are quite happy picking up their favourite tipple at the supermarket and nobody has a problem with that. This is more focused on competing with the mail order companies who send brochures out claiming that the seller has known a particular wine-making family for years. So rather than read second hand that someone knows the family, you get to engage with them yourself.

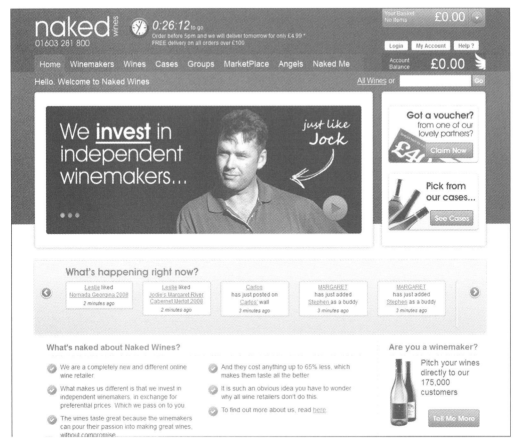

Source: www.nakedwines.com page used with permission of Naked Wines.

Like minds

Peer recommendations make a powerful difference and start to add up to a genuinely personal-feeling service. It starts with the idea that the other customers who insist on communicating with the artisans are going to be like-minded to an extent. They will therefore care what other people have thought about the wines these people actually produce.

So you get to rate the wines you've bought online. Krajewski explains: 'It's one thing us saying, buy this wine, it's delicious, we recommend it, but it's another thing if the customer comes on to the site and they can see 93 percent of 5,121 people would buy this again.'

It starts to sound a bit like the sort of review you might pick up from the aforementioned Amazon for a book, but it can go a little further. Apply this model to books for example. Rather than going and buying a stock of books, the author publishes the first two chapters of a book online and then asks what readers think. The readers come back through an intermediary, who collates the results and says 'yes, they'd be happy to buy this, they'll pay £12 and would rather go straight to paperback than worry about a hardback. So if we buy 1000 from you at £6 each do we have a deal?' The author can then assess the time and costs and work out whether this is viable but the readers, you'll note, have had a say in whether the book gets produced at all.

Sell the idea first, the wine second

Part of the trick of applying a model like this is to simplify, simplify, simplify. This is some-thing that any new social commerce business should learn. If you are looking to consider something similar, you should bear in mind that it can take time to become established and frankly, for the target customer to 'get it.'

Nine months into the business, Naked Wines was still busy explaining how it worked to lots of new customers and prospects. A breakthrough happened when the business started offering half-cases as a taster. Gormley explained: 'We said to people, look, here are six bottles of wine made by winemakers our other customers have funded. If you like them, become an Angel for £20 a month.' Crucially the old trick of knocking out a second rate cheap case to get people's interest is redundant. In this and any other social business, in which feedback will be taken very seriously, the 'acquisition case' or acquisition offer has to be as good as the regular offering.

The figures stack up. At the time of writing, in mid 2011, about half the customers who buy a case of wine become more involved as wine angels, while a high participation figure of

44% leave feedback and comment on the wines. Gormley explained: 'Originally only 9% added their comments. We changed it to a button asking them whether they'd buy a wine again and why. 44% responded, and 17% added more detailed comments. So there's a lot more feedback.'

Not just for wine

Of course, this business is built on people feeling they're getting personal recommendations, built on like-minded people's preferences for wines. The same principle can apply to any other product bought and reviewed by peers in this way. The people who rate, who take part, really feel they're part of the thing, they're in contact with the end producer, and this is why they keep coming back. Amazon pulls off the same trick with books and makes recommendations based on ratings; can your business do the same thing?

If it can, then this is a model that can improve the customer's experience overall. In the case of Naked Wines the social model eliminates the experience of buying a mixed case of wine in a supermarket or a warehouse, during which you find there are two or three wines you really liked, two or three you didn't, and the rest were OK. By reporting back on your tastes and the business having the right algorithm in place on its website it should be possible, the company believes, to all but eliminate any you don't think are superb.

Krajewski monitors the reactions on Twitter – another way of getting a lot of feedback (and it's possible to arrange to Tweet all of your wine recommendations to friends, so they can compare tastes). 'I often see Tweets that say, I was happy bumbling along buying my wine in the supermarket and now you've ruined that for me because now I've had two or three cases from you,' she says. 'They can't possibly go back to the supermarket because they get that consistency and they start to discover the kind of stuff that they like.' The Facebook page also allows for a lot of interaction in longer bursts.

Source: www.facebook.com/nakedwines page used with permission of Naked Wines. Facebook and the Facebook logo are trademarks of Facebook, Inc.

Flexibility: interacting where you want

Yes, staff. Although there's no shop front there is a member of staff attached to each customer for wine advice by phone if they want it – clearly this book is about social commerce but sometimes personal service has to be precisely that.

This raises the idea of melding the internal and external social media feeds. The company has its own Twitter feed and Facebook page. So how, then, do they marry this together with their own highly socialized but private network? 'Well it's just another place to have a conversation and to update our customers on what we're up to, to share information and winemakers to offer their opinion,' says Krajewski. 'We'll often put polls out on Facebook and Twitter. We will let customers know if we need funding for a particular wine or wine-maker. So, you know, it's somewhere to get to know them as well. And so customers just love coming on and saying, tried this last night, absolutely loved it and, you know, there's pictures of their wines and dinner parties. And so it's just an added extra really.'

You can usefully take a step back and consider how this might work in another business. A customer posts a picture of your product or service in action and says how satisfied they are. This gets seen by a whole bunch of people who trust the poster's judgment.

It's difficult to imagine that sort of advertising arriving without substantial payment in any other way. It's useful to note that the company is happy to engage people where they are and wherever they feel comfortable talking. Other businesses have tried and failed to get people from Twitter onto a company site where money will change hands; if the customer wants to go they'll have gone already.

Other social elements are on the site as well. Customers can sync their Gmail, Yahoo! and Microsoft Outlook databases – with safeguards and confidentiality – to see whether any of their friends are already on the wine angel network. 'So you can say instead of 94 out of 105 people liked this wine, hey, Fran liked this wine,' says Gormley. It's worth stressing very loudly at this point that anyone can make their account completely private and not search-able if they wish – but they're likely to miss out on a lot of the fun.

Developing a theme

Once a business has started using the social model other ideas should start to emerge, not just about selling existing products but also about product development, research, and probably other areas.

Take some of Naked Wines' ideas. One plan is to get people noting where they've had really, really good wines in restaurants – to try to persuade the restaurants in question to offer discounts in exchange for increased bookings and then to find where the wines came from.

If they are widely available then Naked Wines, which doesn't like to compete on price, is unlikely to stock them; however, as Krajewski says, if it's a little wine supplier in Cornwall and that's the only place you can get it, they may be able to offer some mutually beneficial business. Clearly, customers choosing the wines on offer is a major way of making the social part of the business very commercial. There may be ways of applying this to other businesses – a customer is encouraged to report back on something in your field which they find useful, and they find it's available from your business after they've requested it. It helps build a sense of community.

A theme you'll find throughout this book is that companies making special offers on their own terms on social media rarely do as well as the ones which listen to what the customer actually wants. Gormley used to work for another wine company and remembers its first time on Twitter, when it offered a 35% discount on a particular case, saying that people could send their email addresses and get a voucher. 'It was like saying, this is all about me,' he says. 'It's best as a pull media. If you're too pushy nothing happens, but if you allow yourself to be gently taken along by the customer when they respond to something it's better.'

It also means taking the rough with the smooth. For example one woman went onto Facebook to complain that Naked Wines were crooks and didn't return money when they said they would. 'In this particular case it was that someone cancelled their Angel account and we refunded their money but it takes three days to get through the banking system, so they went overdrawn while waiting for their 20 quid to come back,' explains Gormley. But when Naked Wines went to respond to this, quick though they were, they found that a number of customers had already been online speaking on its behalf and pointing this out. Get your engagements right and customers will undoubtedly become your best advocates. A public relations person I know works for a major camera manufacturer and has a policy of never commenting on blogs or review sites which are hostile to the products, first because the business doesn't want to be perceived as defensive and second because she is aware that committed customers often start defending the cameras unprompted. This, since they have no vested interests, carries more weight than someone from the PR department replying – so the social model takes over.

Misrepresentation

It will be clear from the Facebook instance described in the Naked Wines case study that it is possible to put notes up about goods or services without declaring an interest. In this instance a woman recommended a competing service for which she in fact worked.

This is a bad idea for a number of reasons. First, if you get caught you look worse than a numpty, you look like a dishonest numpty. Second, it now falls foul of Advertising Standards rulings.

These became quite stringent in 2011. Not only must you declare whether you have an interest in a commercial promotion (many public relations executives get around this by inserting the word 'client' in brackets after a Tweet, Facebook message, or Google Plus update – nobody minds as long as there is disclosure) but your customers should too.

This can make it tricky. One interviewee in this book – and I'm not saying which because they abandoned the practice – at one point offered extra discounts for positive reviews on social networks. This would now fall foul under the current rulings unless someone spells out that they have been incentivized to make the review a positive one, at which stage most people will stop taking it seriously.

Just about the only way around this is to allow reviews both positive and negative to grow naturally.

Watch out for people misrepresenting themselves. One person put a note up on Naked Wine's Facebook page asking what people thought of a particular wine. People responded positively, except one individual who insisted the delivery times and quality from a competitor were better. Gormley thought this was odd and Googled her. She had a blog, and her 'about me' section on this blog said she worked for a Naked Wines competitor.

Gormley asked on Facebook whether she was the same person who ran the blog and worked for another company; her Facebook account and blog vanished very quickly. Whether any damage was done or custom lost to Naked Wines is impossible to track; businesspeople just have to be aware that this stuff can happen.

Mostly existing customers will be honest and open – and if they really don't like a service or product they're entitled to say so. You'll need to deal with it, learn from it, and move on. Get the product or service right and many will volunteer their enthusiasm and give you an excellent write-up for the newer customers to read.

In with the old, in with the new

Acquiring new customers can be an expensive business, and the costs should tumble when a social means is utilized.

First have a think about the usual business models in your trade. Perhaps you're used to sending out fliers (fix that cost in your mind). Obviously not everybody responds to a flier and your sales are likely to be in the single percentages – so the cost of acquiring a customer goes up. So could you be doing something else with that money?

Let's relate that back to the Naked Wines example and see how it works. Consider, if you're a buyer by the case, how many fliers you get through the door; someone has to pay £1 for each of those pieces of mail. A really good response to a mailshot – and the wine industry does well – is about 6% of people buying, so about one in 16 people will buy a case.

This means every case sold in that promotion has cost £16 in direct marketing materials, so if the case being bought is on promotion and costs £50 then there's only room for £34 worth of wine, bottling, packaging, taxes. Naked Wines eliminates the mailshots by the very simple expedient of giving a voucher to everyone who buys a case to give away.

These vouchers – usually £50 – can't be used by the person who bought the wine, they go instead to new customers. These might be friends of the buyer, they might be colleagues, they might be random people on Twitter or Facebook (just try offering £50 of no-strings-attached wine to your friends if they enjoy the stuff and see how popular you become very quickly) – and crucially the amount of people who re-order after their first discounted case is about two-thirds. Giving a voucher for £50, which clearly is based on the retail price rather than the cost to Naked Wines, makes acquisition of new customers very cost effective indeed – and once again it's possible exclusively because of the amount of electronic communication involved. If the friend for whom you've reserved the case is in a position to buy quickly, the new customer can be fully acquired within seconds of the voucher appearing on the existing customer's screen.

Technology and legality

Clearly none of this can be achieved without a basic grasp of some pretty strong technology. This isn't a book on how to build a website – there are plenty of those around. The most important thing you can do from your own site in social terms, other than analyze the reviews and see what's doing well (also analyzing sales to see what's moving and what isn't as you'd do with any other business) is to identify and welcome the returning customer and understand their habits. This is done through cookies. These are the bits of technology that allow your computer to recognize a returning customer when they come and see you again.

Cookies, straightforwardly, are little bits of code in your website that go out to your customers and sit on their computers. They tell a business's system that it's a returning customer and who it is; this is how you get sites like Amazon saying 'Hi (your name), here are some recommendations based on what you've ordered before.' The cookie is the piece of code that's told Amazon it's you, simple as that.

The Cookie Code

If you need to know, they look like this:

```
<script type="text/javascript">cookieSet();</script>
```

This tells the Javascript on your website to send a cookie to the customer's computer. A quick Google search tells me the website should also have the following code in the <header> area:

```
var cookieText = "Put your desired cookie value here";
var cookiePrefix = "";
var myPage = location.href;
var wwwFlag = myPage.indexOf('www');
if (wwwFlag > 0) {
cookiePrefix = "www";
}
var cookieName = cookiePrefix + "cbCookie";
function cookieSet(){
if (document.cookie != document.cookie) {
index = document.cookie.indexOf(cookieName);
} else {
index = -1;
} if (index == -1) {
document.cookie=cookieName+"="+cookieText+"cbEndCookie;
expires=Monday, 04-Apr-2020 05:00:00 GMT";
}
}
```

. . . and my head's bleeding already, how about yours? If you're into coding you'll be able to check that lot. If you're briefing a web designer then you'll need to alert them about using cookies.

The law has changed regarding cookies. You can't just assume they'll be OK with customers any more, you need to make sure you have the client signed up to the idea that you're going to be sending them along. This is to prevent abuses and people sending things to customer computers without telling them.

Laudable though this might appear it does have disadvantages. American sites, quite reasonably, are unaffected by British and European laws, so they don't feel as bound to request permission before sending cookies to customers. So they don't bother asking, so customers don't know. They're harmless enough and nobody is doing anything crooked but you might find that customers who've read about identity theft and the like will refuse to have you putting something on their system.

It is what we call in the trade a right nuisance and an area in which we are completely out of step with American law, giving our homegrown businesses an inbuilt disadvantage. It is also European law and something about which we can do precisely nothing.

Action points

The people at Naked Wines are an engaging bunch and there's a lot for other businesses to learn from their business model. What's noticeable is that their customers feel part of the business; this really is social media turning into social commerce and feeling that they have joined something. Gormley and his colleagues were already steeped in the world of wine selling and really knew their stuff. Sourcing what they perceive as new and unique products is something that has to be done by going out and visiting people – there isn't a 'social media' or 'social commerce' way of doing this.

Making it pay, though, and making deals happen which otherwise couldn't, is something social media are doing very well. It's also allowing the digitally-aware customer to communicate with and engage with his or her suppliers in the way he or she chooses; there's really no point in insisting everyone goes to your Facebook page if they're happier on Twitter or on your own website.

Naked Wines has this group ethos written into its DNA. It's how it started. In the next chapter we'll look at fast ways of getting social commerce into an established business and ways of making it pay. Meanwhile here are some specific pointers:

- Use social media, whether on your site or elsewhere, to give customers a say in the development of your products and what you actually sell. They will buy into the idea if they feel they have a stake.

- Encourage customers to choose the products, to make them feel very well looked after.

- Set systems to note the customer's individual landing page or a customer's previous behaviour and buying patterns on the site, then tailor offers to those behaviours.

- Base new offerings and the products on the customer's individual landing page on previous behaviours. This will almost certainly allow them to feel that a service or product set is for them.

- Get your customers recruiting from each other to help add to the personalization of the experience. Get them to buy into a service or set of goods like this and you'll find they become one of your best advocates online.

- Find suitable prompts to encourage customers to review things. Responding to prompts to buy or at least try something from people you know is bound to perform better than responding to someone with vested interests in the purchase taking place.

- Use cookie technology so that your systems know what your customers did last time they were on your site – and address them by name.

2 DIVING IN

As this book progresses you'll read about people who have done new and innovative things using social media to ramp up their commercial presence. Some have used the social commerce model directly and some have not. You'll read about a brewery that raised hundreds of thousands of new capital investment simply by asking its social media followers to send it – and by going through an awful lot of regulatory stuff and revamping its website whilst ensuring it was legally watertight at the same time. It did this largely by itself.

You'll also find out about the agency that helped a worldwide hotel chain engage with its potential employees by putting a game together, the computer company that made millions (literally) which it could track directly back to its Twitter site, and the solicitor that used Twitter to give away freebies, whilst still maintaining an utterly professional presence.

These companies had resources at their disposal. They had established relationships with web developers, they had critical mass and the timing was right.

This chapter isn't aimed at them.

This chapter is aimed at the sort of person who knows there's something going on in social commerce. The sort of person who understands there is a distinct advantage to harnessing the Internet and the mass of customers who could be looking for their service but who don't quite know where to start. The sort of person who wants an easy way of trying it out, of seeing whether it's likely to work, or whether it's just marketing baloney.

This chapter is about diving in, getting into the social commerce arena quickly, usually in partnership with someone else, and taking advantage of their efforts. It's about using skills that are already there, it's about making your social commerce presence felt very quickly indeed.

In reading this chapter you will take away:

- Means of turning your company into a social commerce operation by using Groupon and similar services – plus the drawbacks and the advantages

- Managing your expectations of this and other services – understanding that volume might not be a great thing every time

- Looking at Facebook Places and how a larger business can take advantage of the scheme

- Looking at FourSquare and how to turn your business into a 'venue'

- Raising capital through social media without having to do everything yourself

- Looking at Google Plus and what that might offer businesses in the future.

Groupon and its ilk

Groupon is one of the biggest players in the instant social commerce market at the moment. By this I mean you don't have to be particularly social yourself; you just sign up and let the company do the work, and take a lot of the cash. That's not a criticism – you want all the cash, you get your own database of customers.

The way it works is very simple indeed. You go to www.grouponworks.co.uk. There are introductory videos there so you can have a look, but basically you sign up online with contact details and some elementary information about your business and what you're selling. Groupon has a team that researches the viability of the idea and whether its customer base will go for it. Assuming that's positive the company sends a contract with commission terms; Groupon finds a slot for you.

The company works by sending out a few daily deals to its client base at www.groupon.co.uk. These are the deals signed at Grouponworks and a timetable gets agreed between Groupon and the business owner. There's a variable split in the amount of income it takes compared to the amount that you get – but basically people who've signed up are offered a deal. If they like it then they buy a voucher and use it to buy their goods. You return the voucher to

Groupon and get your share, just as you would with any other voucher scheme. Groupon has a team dealing with queries and customers but mostly they come to the owner of the business rather than the seller of the voucher if there is any sort of problem.

Easy? OK, it should be and there's no reason why this shouldn't work spectacularly well if a bit of business and common sense are applied early on.

Managing expectations

In the early days of this scheme there was almost no way of telling how popular it would become. A lot of people forecast that the response would be much lower than it actually ended up being and found they were unable to fulfil the demand. For example, a work colleague who is a tailor was telling me why he'd never work with Groupon. When he went for a haircut the phone didn't stop ringing and as a result, the haircut took longer than usual. He asked why this was and the barber said 'Groupon – the phone just hasn't stopped, and I'm booking people months in advance.'

Others have found the market which it reaches is wrong for their business. A luxury Italian villa contacted whilst producing this book told me 'They set a low price, take half and deliver dross customers. Bye!' He did add 'We did much better from people who saw the Groupon ads, refused to give them credit cards and booked at full rates for longer.'

You can start to get a bit of a fixed impression about this business, but there are two points to take away from these examples. Lesson one: allow for a good response rate. In example two let's modify the 'dross customers' to 'inappropriate for the business' customers – which is probably more accurate. Again, with the business being longer established you could probably find out more about its likely catchment areas.

Helen Bradley is co-owner of upmarket hairdresser MacLeod Bradley in South Manchester and she tried Groupon to get some more customers when it first started. The offer was a highly discounted colour, cut, and treatment. Bradley sold more than 200 vouchers but admitted that although 'It was a very new idea, I wouldn't say it went amazingly well.'

Hang on. You go into something with the idea of getting loads of new customers and the response is massive – what went wrong? Although the deal attracted a massive amount of people, it was actually targeting a different market from that which the salon wanted. As an upmarket establishment, the clientele they wanted to attract and retain was not the kind of clientele that were buying the hugely cheaper deals. So despite having a surge in sales, only a handful of customers returned to the salon once the deal was over.

So in this particular example, price was an issue. This is an upmarket salon where people happily pay £150 for a full service including a colour, cut, and everything else. Selling that for £20–£30 as Groupon did was always going to bring people in but would it do much else?

Sanity check: selling for full price

Many businesses make a mistake with promotions like Groupon. You might use it to get people through the door and think it doesn't matter if you're making a loss because they'll come back and spend at full price. This is probably wrong in most cases.

Let's look at the social pitch behind Groupon and companies like it. It asks participating companies to knock their prices down and of course it takes a reasonable cut at the same time. The customer doesn't see this – they simply see a 70%-off deal or something coming into their in-box. This doesn't mean they're willing or able to pay the full price.

Take a real example. Just as this book was going to press, a tailor – not one of the ones mentioned in another chapter – was offering a bespoke suit for £495 – that's fully hand made to measure. The full price, however, was £1,239. Simple common sense dictates that the fact someone is reasonably affluent and will treat themselves to a £495 suit for special occasions doesn't necessarily put them into the £1000+ per suit bracket. So many of the new

> customers simply won't come back. It's not difficult to understand; it happens in end-of-year or mid-season sales as well – customers who buy designer clothes at those points often wouldn't dream of paying the full price for them.
>
> The lesson which can be extrapolated is that the initial offer, regardless of how discounted it is, has to have some margin left in it so that it acts as a positive thing in its own right. If your idea is to bring new people into the business, good luck – but it may not work.

The good news is that you can make these deals work for you and your business as long as you assert control, and only accept deals that are achievable and equitable. Kary Stewart heads up digital production company Ignite Creative in London. She had run as many as three Groupon deals as this book went to press, for discounted training in film and photography. She was prompted to use the service when publicly-funded courses started to reduce in numbers so she had to go to the private sector.

She did her research first and was aware of the pitfalls that people like Bradley had uncovered, including oversubscription, which is the most common difficulty. You can find a lot of advice by checking Google for 'Groupon experience' (or 'LivingSocial' experience or any of the other competition). 'I added contractual terms like time constraints, availability and demand constraints so I had parameters people were aware of, which covered me.'

It shouldn't reflect on people using the service earlier that they weren't aware these things were going to be necessary. Stewart also catered for undersubscription – contractually, if only two people had signed up for a particular date she wasn't obliged to run the class. She also stipulated online bookings only, so that the phone didn't ring off the hook as it did for others before her.

The discount on offer from Ignite Creative was around 70% off a normal course fee. Groupon took about 40% of the commission but after VAT this turned into around 50%. This could leave someone with an absolute pittance – a 70% discount leaves 30%, less half means that Stewart was faced with selling her courses for 15% of the usual price. She was determined not to make it a loss leader, though. 'I checked my profit margins and calculated my overheads, and definitely went into it with a view to making a profit. Not a huge one, it was about volume.' When she was serving the public sector she would typically run four or five of these courses a year, which equated to a maximum of 200 people per annum. 'With Groupon you're selling easily 1000 so you're running five times the amount of courses, which brings your overheads down. Hiring facilities comes down because there are more courses, for example.'

Returning business was one of the objectives and . . . it hasn't happened. There are a number of reasons – see the box – but it certainly vindicated the reasoning behind every course having to pay for itself in and of itself. As a result she'll happily run the scheme again.

Location-based services: Facebook and FourSquare

Groupon and its counterparts are based on getting people to come to your business in the first place but there's very little in them to encourage loyalty particularly. This is fair enough; the companies themselves aren't claiming that's what they're in it for; they want to get new people to come to your door.

For loyalty there are online versions of the loyalty card to which you can look. Loyalty cards themselves like Nectar are certainly usable for many online transactions. There are other online-only services, though, which have caught the imagination of the online communities in ways that the standard card people won't because they're perceived as not being part of that world.

Facebook Places

Facebook Places is a pretty straightforward scheme; a substantial brand signs up for Facebook Places, people visit it and check in with their phones, and from that point on it's like a social network-based loyalty scheme exclusively based around a business's location. You get points, you get vouchers, and you're encouraged to go back and visit the same place more than once. Facebook Places is better suited to the larger company and indeed its price structure means it's not going to appeal to many corner shop retail premises.

Yo! Sushi, the international chain of Japanese food restaurants, had been aware for a while that its clientele was very technologically savvy when Mark McCulloch became head of marketing and he wanted the brand to become more proactive and to take control.

An American company had attracted a lot of members to its Facebook site by offering free starters to anyone who joined and acquired half a million people very quickly; McCulloch was keen to avoid the so-called 'voucher hounds' who'll sign up for the free food and not engage with the brand.

With the help of social media agency Punktilio, Yo! Sushi was among the first companies involved when the UK version of the Facebook Places scheme was being launched. It's worth bearing in mind at this point that Facebook was throwing £400,000 of PR at this launch, and highlighting Yo! Sushi and other businesses meant that the results were always going to be very positive. Yo! Sushi had agreed to give away 2000 meals to the value of £35 approx. People had to check into a participating restaurant – the canny ones did it well before they turned up – with their phones and the Facebook app, and this would check their location and give them a 'golden ticket.' This would act like a voucher with a unique code which matched a code in the till systems at the branch, so that the offer could be claimed. McCulloch was around at the time: 'I was there at three o'clock, which is usually a dead time in restaurants, and basically in Nottingham, there were queues round the block,' he says. All 2000 meals in the offer went within 24 hours.

This sort of marketing backup has to be paid for somehow and after the launch Facebook made the decision that to take part in its Places scheme would now cost new businesses £50,000. This effectively puts the lid on it for small businesses.

FourSquare

This is another location-based service but has a much lower barrier to entry than the Facebook equivalent. It is a matter of signing up, agreeing the deal, and keeping it open – think of it as Groupon with a vastly smaller discount but an ongoing one. It's therefore likely to work best for businesses which are comfortable with offering a discount rather than anything too 'premium' or which works on achieving a consistent RRP.

FourSquare behaves slightly differently from most social media in that it already has many businesses listed. Go to foursquare.com/business and click the link for business owners. Search for your business with an approximate location. If it's there you can click the 'claim your business' button, register with the site, and go from there setting up whichever promotions you like. If not, click 'add a new venue to Foursquare' and add your details there.

You can then start setting deals for anyone who wanders in with a smartphone that has its location services enabled and FourSquare among its apps. They start to play an extended game, in which whoever walks into your premises the most gets to be the Mayor and other ranks.

Do I look cool in this?

One thing you'll need to bear in mind about the customer who takes part in the location-based marketing schemes is that they will announce their presence every time they walk into your venue and this is likely to be repeated through their Twitter stream. Assuming you run a coffee shop that's fine, restaurants do well too.

There are also – and I'm putting this as politely as I can – less exciting retail premises which nevertheless can get attention. Businesses should only sign up if they're certain their clientele will want to share their location with their friends. During the writing of this book I saw one senior public relations manager have as his update on Twitter that he had just become Mayor of Tesco Express, Crouch End (or wherever he lived). He was of course ribbed something rotten about getting a life; that said, it's got Tesco a mention in this book!

This 'announcing where you are' thing is probably why no lap dancing clubs are known to have signed up yet.

Transactions on Facebook

Logically, if you accept that the people to whom you're trying to sell have moved to the social networks and are less likely to want to interact on your site, you should move your actual transactions onto a social network. This has many implications for the way you talk to people and what you expect them to do on your site but it has worked for a number of companies which have set up actual transactions on their Facebook pages. ASOS, the fashion company, will be pleased to sell you a pair of shoes on its website of course, but if you want to stay on Facebook and buy something there that isn't a problem. There's a page on which you can do precisely that.

This "Facebook Commerce" is an idea which is taking unexpected turns. What do you do, for example, if your car's windscreen gets chipped? Pick up the phone and find out how damned much it's going to cost by talking to a garage or windscreen specialist (which for most is, I assume, the standard response) – or rush to Facebook?

Windscreen specialist Autoglass has found that people are indeed going to Facebook with their car-related window problems. Marketing director David Meliveo says the journey to putting a Facebook app in place started between two and three years before it went live. Like every brand, Autoglass had become aware that social media was becoming increasingly important in its clients' lives. 'We started thinking about what our goal should be in social media, but before that we started trying to understand what impact the social media would have on brands and businesses,' he says. The company started by establishing tools to measure the impact of social media and spent a year and a half listening and watching what people were saying.

One finding of note was that on Facebook there was a lot of interest in the Autoglass brand and people were starting to follow individual Autoglass technicians. It really ramped up when a TV advertising campaign kicked off focusing on a fictional technician called Gavin – suddenly there were Facebook groups with tens of thousands of members talking about this Gavin bloke. Mostly, though, the engagement was about listening to feedback, addressing negativity when it arose, and watching for brand abuse.

It became apparent that social media were impacting customer service, pricing, customers' first contact with the company, the legal department, sales, and most obviously marketing. It's worth any business with a substantial brand considering the process that Autoglass went through; around 18 months just considering the impact and how customers would like to interact is a long time. The discovery that the new media were so pivotal to so many departments within the organization had a profound effect on the attitude to what could previously have been written off as a fad.

The next logical step was to 'take it proactive.' Some people wanted to have a bit of fun with the brand, some wanted to interact with technicians, and some wanted more facilities to report their needs online.

The Facebook app

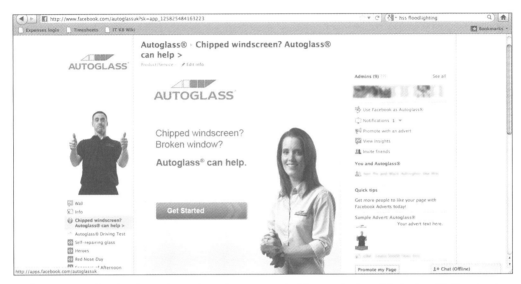

Source: www.facebook.com/autoglassuk page used with permission of Autoglass®. Facebook and the Facebook logo are trademarks of Facebook, Inc.

As this book went to press Autoglass had put its Facebook app online for only a couple of months. The idea was based not only on research into what Facebook could do but also on what people were doing with social media in general. FourSquare was attracting businesses offering discounts based on walking into a venue and retailers – as mentioned already with the ASOS example – were selling items. A sub-group of customers are starting to orient their online lives around Facebook and expecting to make transactions happen there as well as go there to interact with friends.

'So we had consumers coming to us and saying, so, when are you going to allow us to start making bookings through Facebook?' says Meliveo.

This is where it gets technical. The first thing it had to do was adjust the API – Application Program Interface – of its own website to allow for the launch of a mobile phone site and a mobile app. 'Once you've developed your API and everything is in one place then you can develop anything you want,' says Meliveo.

Underpinning this were years of effort in improving the website so that more and more people looking at it were converted to customers – this is standard business practice but it was important. The company took the learnings from the website, from the mobile site, and from the Android and iPhone apps it had developed with the rewritten API but then created something on Facebook from scratch.

'The first step was to find the right developer,' says Meliveo. 'Within our business we didn't have anyone with the right skills for the API work and for a Facebook app, so we had to find a couple of specialists.' The company scoped the project and found that after the API and necessary back office work it took around six weeks to develop the front end of the app – the bit the consumer sees. 'Facebook was helpful, they didn't make it difficult at all; the work was in linking with our back office and making sure the app linked in with our reservation system.'

Beyond the development the success of the app depends on marketing. Autoglass was still faced with a mind set from clients that didn't necessarily say 'I've got a problem with my windscreen, I must log on to Facebook.' They did want choice, though; interacting through phone, website, apps, Facebook – they wanted all the options. 'The key for us was to be present wherever the customer was,' confirms Meliveo.

It's an ongoing process and of course feedback from consumers is vital. They ask 'have you done this, have you considered this' and some excellent ideas are coming through. Early signs were that the response would be phenomenal; 5000 users or more had a look at the app within the first couple of weeks including new customers and bookings were coming through.

So, would your customers respond to an app? Are they on Facebook themselves and do they effectively live there while they're online? If a company the size of Autoglass had to recruit developers specially, you're unlikely to have the in-house skills to do it yourself. Either recruit a specialist or find an external company with specific API/Facebook integration skills – it isn't a light undertaking. There isn't an easy, shrinkwrapped sell-through-Facebook package – no doubt someone will come up with one. Leading people back to your own e-commerce site or a supplier of your goods was the best option for non-programmers as this book went to press, although there is a risk of alienating customers who find the change of site jarring.

Location-based services aren't the only thing possible on social media of course. How about raising money?

Give us a fiver – raising social capital through social media

In the next chapter I'll be looking at the different communities you can address through social means, turning your business into a social commerce enterprise on many different levels. One of those is the investor community. It's possible to talk to tiny investors and get a whole lot of them to put money in. There is of course a lot of spadework in advance.

The example in that chapter, Brewdog, did it all themselves including getting all of the professional advice they needed, and you'll need to do the same. But you may not have to do everything through your website; as in the Groupon example, there are services that will package up your request for funding and present it to potential investors on your behalf, collect the money for you, and hold it in escrow until you have enough of a lump sum to issue the shares. It's like an episode of 'Dragons' Den' in which you're presenting to thousands rather than five people, and if they only have 50 quid each to invest they can do so.

One of the earliest entrants into this market is Crowdcube. Co-founder Darren Westlake set the business up as a reaction to the difficulty of finding investment in the start-ups in which he had been involved. What if, he thought, you could crowd-source the business angel model, by which investors could put money in en masse?

'I came up with the idea of crowd funding in late 2008/early 2009. There was – and is – a company called Sellaband. It enabled you to put a small amount of money into a band.' He simply thought if you could get a load of enthusiasts together for bands you could do the same thing for business.

The area is of course regulated within an inch of its life, so he brought a firm of solicitors in and eventually thrashed out a model which is compliant with all of the financial regulations. The company had the go-ahead from the Financial Services Association in February 2011.

As readers will imagine, since the business is based on issuing shares and impressing upon potential investors that there is a return to be had, a lot of the work happens before you reach the website.

Preparation and application

The first thing Crowd Cube looks for – and by no means does every business registering interest get listed on the site – is a solid business plan. This has to include financial forecasts. 'By asking people for those we filter down a lot of requests substantially, because although they would love to start their own business they're not investment ready,' says Westlake.

Business plan and forecasts being in a format that can be uploaded, the next stage is to fill in a form on the crowdcube.com website with basic details of the business and what it aims to do. Crowdcube then takes a few days to read the documentation.

Tell us more about your proposed pitch...

If you have a great for a project that you want to get funding for then please complete the proposed pitch form below. We'll review your application and get back to you as soon as possible.

Funding title:

Description:

This information is for internal use only and is not made public. Please provide as much information as possible about your proposed pitch. The information submitted will be used to approve or decline your pitch. If we need more information about your pitch, we'll contact you by email.

If your proposed pitch is approved you'll be asked to create a full detailed pitch for our website that will be made public. It will include: description, video pitch, images and supporting documents.

Name:

City:

Country:

Phone:

E-mail:

Funding required (£):

Supporting documents: Choose File   No file chosen

☐ I accept terms and conditions

Source: www.crowdcube.com/submit-pitch page used with permission of Eureka Communications.

The vetting process is in fact quite vigorous and fewer than one in ten get listed. As well as the business planning, Crowdcube scrutinizes the people involved, the history of the business and any existing management accounts, and whether the 'crowd' is likely to be interested. Solid though some businesses may be, if it looks dull then it's unlikely to attract a lot of interest so – with some regret – it may not reach the site. There will inevitably be questions and clarifications, then after an email dialogue there will be a yes or a no.

Assuming your business is one of the minority that gets a yes, the Crowdcube team clicks a button in the back office that opens up a pitch editing system so that you can put your offering online. This pitch should include a description of the business and the team. There's an option to put YouTube video up – stats show that people with video do better than those without – and images and anything else you think might help.

Businesses also need a deadline by which their target must be met. This was six months initially and it's likely to have shrunk by the time this book comes out because of the way people have invested; typically there is a flurry at the beginning and at the end but a lull in the middle. This means that if an investor puts money in early they won't hear until five or six months later whether their investment is going into the company or is going to be returned.

If you don't get enough investment by the deadline the money already put forward is returned to the small investors. This is why in Westlake's view the hard work actually starts when the pitch is published. 'One part of the vetting process is that we ask you how you're going to promote the pitch,' he says. 'This is key to its success, it's a partnership between ourselves and the entrepreneur. We encourage our entrepreneurs to use social media to promote their pitches to investors already on the site and their own target audiences.' Suppliers, customers, friends, family – the idea is to get it to go viral.

The pitches with the most success so far have been those who've put the most into the promotion, he says. The first successful investment, Bubble and Balm, was confirmed within months of Crowdcube setting up, announcing a £75,000 investment through 82 investors buying 10% of the company. Investments varied between £10 and £7500. The second, Personal Development Bureau, reached its phase one target of £25,000 shared between 45 investors within weeks.

There are clear messages from the experience of the businesses involved so far. Don't assume it's an easy option. The business plan needs to be as solid as if you were talking to an experienced business angel investor. Marketing your pitch is down to you as much as it's down to Crowdcube – the company will help but it's your business and an investment you're seeking, so the financial structuring and getting word into the market is up to you.

What, you thought there was a magic button for getting cash into your business . . . ?

Footnote for the future: Google Plus

As this book went to press, Google came out with its second attempt at a social media offering, Google Plus. One of the first things it did was to go through and weed out all of the members who were businesses rather than personal accounts. Its efforts were imperfect and incomplete; it took out one magazine's corporate presence but left all the staff in place, for example.

This time it's gained more traction. It's pretty certain that Google will do something business-specific but as yet it's not clear what; given that the company has maps as well as the biggest search engine in the business it would be reasonable to expect location-based services to be among the offerings.

Action points

There has been a lot to take in during this chapter. First, the idea that a mass market is necessarily a permanent one needs to be run through a reality checker before it spreads too far and wide. Groupon, a lot of people have found, delivers many new one-off customers but, as I've discussed, there's no evidence to suggest that someone will buy or indeed that they have the income to buy a full-price item they've just bought at 70% off.

There's also the fact that a mass of people may not be the right market for your product or offering. This doesn't mean they're 'dross' customers but the wrong customers for your particular product. Get the balance right and there's a huge marketing advantage to be had by going social. Likewise finding the right backers by appealing to the crowd; you may need patience and not all investments will work out. If you welcome customers to your locations you could also consider the location-based services; Facebook Places is likely to be unaffordable unless it changes its policy but FourSquare isn't.

- Consider the sites covered in this chapter as a means of helping first. If it takes off and you have the technological skill or a suitable web design contact you can always take it in-house later.

- Look at the demographic your chosen partner serves and consider whether they will actually deliver the clients you're after. Understand the implications of any promotion, digital or otherwise, that you want to be involved in.

- Remember to ensure your pricing will get you a good enough margin in and of itself – assume no customers will come back at full price.

- Check whether there's already anything being done using your name and get the networks to help take it down for you.

- Raising money for a small business is difficult but there are small investors who will be interested in backing the right company for a stake in something before it goes listed. This is a realistic group of people to target for money.

- Write a business plan and forecast your business income if you want backing from anyone at all, even if some of your backers are only going to put in a tenner.

- Look at Facebook apps if your clients are on that network. Remember you'll need significant web skills, including rewriting APIs, and will have to write the app from the ground up.

3 GETTING NEW CUSTOMERS IN THE SOCIAL MEDIA AGE

I f I'd been writing a book like this 15 years ago it wouldn't have been about social media – I mean, I was using stuff I would now call social media but the term itself didn't exist at that stage. I was a tech journalist so I was using all sorts of things before they really took off and went mainstream – it's the nature of the job.

For most of the business world, 15 years ago the questions weren't about how they interacted with their customers but 'should we have a website' and 'is email worth the effort or is it just a passing fad.' No, look, really, it wasn't a given. They got through that and then made the terrible discovery that just putting a website up there didn't mean that loads of customers would suddenly turn up.

This was a bit of a shock to a lot of people. The initial hype around the Internet was very clear: if you were a small computer seller somewhere in a shed you'd be able to compete with the mighty Dell overnight (we'll be hearing from Dell later in this chapter). This was of course a pile of old nonsense; if, say, Amazon could afford a massive warehouse of books, CDs, and videos (not DVDs at that stage) and take out full page adverts in magazines, on London tube platforms, and elsewhere then they were always going to have better reach and fulfilment than their smaller counterparts.

If we leap back to the present day then we have the same thing happening again to an extent. The smaller businesses heard that they could interact with their customers and a lot of them got very excited. Many forgot that they'd have to get their clients to their social media feeds in the first place, and then keep them entertained. The prospects would be even more difficult.

This chapter is about those new customers and getting them to respond. It's about turning the 'social' side of your business into 'commerce' – otherwise why bother?

It's about smaller businesses – I'll be talking to A Suit That Fits in Bermondsey. It's about larger businesses too, Dell is included as a smaller, second case study in a few pages (not because it's an unimportant company but because my guess is fewer readers will expect their business to reach that size any time soon. Or if they do, they're not going to expect to get there on the strength of a £12.99 book. You need at least two books for that.)

In this chapter you'll have a look at:

- Attracting a customer or client's attention in the first place

- Making sure customers and prospects really feel engaged and that they are getting a personal service

- Strategies that have worked, strategies that haven't

- Getting feedback from customers when your business feels remote from them.

Hey you, want a bargain?

The obvious way for any marketer to attract someone's attention and get them to come and buy from you is through an advertisement. The equivalent on social media would be a Tweet, LinkedIn update, Google Plus notice depending on how those work out over time, or Facebook page entry, preferably with something a bit promotional on it.

Sometimes they'd be right and sometimes they'd be wrong. A lot of companies have come in for criticism for doing nothing but announcing offers on their pages and feeds. Worse, they can invade privacy however well intentioned. Here are some howlers people have made, gleaned from websites (which I've credited).

- Announce the competition – then don't announce a winner

  A blogger at Bosmol.com points out that if people enter a competition and don't win, they expect to know who did. This has two unlooked-for effects. First if you don't name a winner they'll think there wasn't a prize and won't join in again, probably won't buy any-thing from you. So you congratulate the prize winner publicly, right? Right-ish! You first put in the competition's terms and conditions that you're going to mention the winner, otherwise they may feel they're having their Twitter/Facebook contacts shared without permission. A tiny point one would hope, but people are very sensitive about privacy on social networks.

- Bore the reader with nothing but promotions

Again Bosmol.com is among the sites pointing out that if you do nothing but promote competitions and deals – unless that's all your business does in which case fair play to you – people will lose attention very quickly indeed. Obviously this is counterproductive in any medium, particularly in one devoted to engagement.

- Hijacking current affairs

In my first book on social media I highlighted an example of a furniture company trying to hijack the 'Iran' hashtag to sell sofas. This was a bad thing and the brand suffered – I assumed it was a one-off, until the riots in Egypt in February 2011, when American designer Kenneth Cole's business tweeted 'Millions are in uproar in #Cairo. Rumor is they heard our new spring collection is now available online . . .'

The backlash was inevitable and the company apologized immediately, although the full text of the Tweet reportedly appeared in one of its store windows for a while.

- Not putting any corporate branding on their Twitter feed

Unbelievably people still run corporate feeds without putting their company logo onto it, as American marketer Rodney Rumford points out on his blog. This is crazy – there is every opportunity to upload a picture of your latest or newest product, or logo, as the background to your profile page. The profile needs filling in too. At the time of publication one of the worst offenders – oddly – was @bbclondon, which is genuine but hadn't taken the trouble to upload any basic information or to use anything but the default Twitter 'egg' for its Twitter picture. This changed to a logo just as we went to press.

- Spamming

One day someone will come up with a definitive answer as to what constitutes Spam on something like Twitter or Facebook. But constant and overly frequent marketing messages and exortations to 'buy my service' probably qualifies and is not recommended.

Personal v business: the Obama Effect

The debate as to whether social networking should be mostly business-oriented or personal when you're writing on behalf of your company is many-faceted. Elsewhere in this book I talk to Innocent, which has a knack of coming out with a consistent corporate voice most of the time which is pretty impressive given the amount of people on the account.

There are times when people Tweet their opinions and seem to forget their customers and clients may not share them. In 2008 during the American Presidential race, Barack Obama got the hang of the importance of Twitter very quickly indeed. He urged people to vote for him (and in the run-up to the crucial vote on the debt ceiling in July 2011 he did the same). It had a stunning effect.

The thing is, as Taplin Web Design in Australia points out through its blog, so did many of his followers, and some forgot they were Tweeting on their business account. So when a business Tweeted out 'Anyone who follows McCain and Palin hates America. What's wrong with you?' the response from many Republican clients was predictably hostile.

These followers are your clients and prospects, not your mates. They might find certain views you hold contrary to their own, and that's allowed. If something isn't in line with your corporate rather than personal beliefs, and it's as sensitive as politics, don't put it on your business social media pages.

Suit you, sir (or madam)

I have a feeling I'm dating myself quite badly with that sub-head. Nonetheless I'm going to write a little about the tailoring industry in this section. We'll come to the interview a little later but for the moment I'd like readers to consider only one thing: the tailoring experience. Not all of you will have been to a tailor but you'll have seen the idea on TV and in magazines – you get measured up, fussed around, you spend thousands (over £2K for a Savile Row suit).

Of course it's cheaper to buy a ready-made, off the peg suit. But there are people who might spend a little more for something more individual and it's these customers who are the focus of the next case study. The initial task, then, is to persuade that customer that it's worth spending the extra money, and social media are one way in which the point can be made.

The first thing you have to do is to attract that particular client's attention. This is where David Hathiramani, joint founder and managing director of A Suit That Fits, has scored pretty highly. The business is a tailoring company but not a traditional one; it's one of the wave of online and partly offline lower-budget tailors that started in the first decade of this century. It wasn't the first but is certainly among the higher-profile due to a concerted marketing effort. It didn't want a swish and expensive shop front from the beginning, and when it began in 2006 Hathiramani and his colleagues were already Facebook members so engaging through social media came naturally. 'We thought the people we were wanting to sell to were like us; the idea was engaging for our kind of age group,' he says.

This isn't a book about clothing but that age group at the time would have been people in their mid-twenties, so they were getting serious jobs and looking less fabulous in teenage fashions but weren't yet in a position to go and spend four figures on a bespoke suit. Part of the eventual mission was to allow them to measure themselves for their own clothes if they felt confident enough, which potentially detracts even further from the service element (although having a tailor measure you is still a service on offer). And this was the first generation to 'go native' in the social networks so there was an easy crossover into the social channels. There was always going to be more than just a company Twitter page.

Hathiramani explains that there is a multi-pronged approach. There is a general company Twitter feed which mentions company information to anyone who may be interested and which highlights blog entries, as anyone would expect. 'There are also kind of fun experiences with photos that may not be high quality pictures but they're good enough for our Twitter feed, so they go there rather than onto our website,' he says.

This actually says something pretty interesting about the Twitter customer's expectation; they don't expect excellent pictorial quality all the time, whereas in this business's perception the website reader will expect something that feels more permanent. So if a celebrity happens to drop in – as happens occasionally – a snapshot might appear in the Twitter feed with permission but if it's not a formal photo shoot there's no expectation it'll be archived permanently.

As he says, this isn't the only Twitter feed for the company. Every style advisor, of whom there are several in the branches, has his or her own Twitter feed prefaced with the initials ASTF – so Hathiramani tweets as ASTFDavid. 'You come to us because generally you like the person who's dealing with you on the other end and we try and get likeable characters to work with us,' he says. 'They're all a little bit eccentric in some way I think and so what we like to do is to kind of showcase their personalities.'

It suits most, although not all, and Twitter isn't compulsory for staff. Engaging rather than selling, however, has many benefits. 'For example, David Minns [branch manager] in Bristol seems to have an ongoing relationship with GQ Magazine on Twitter which is quite neat because he posts things there, we Tweet him and they get on well with each other.' This suits him and other style advisors Tweet in different ways. 'It's a good way of our customers actually seeing the personality of the style advisor before booking in,' says Hathiramani.

Individual tones

Source: www.facebook.com/aSuitTF page used with permission of A Suit That Fits. Facebook and the Facebook logo are trademarks of Facebook, Inc.

This combination of personalization with a corporate flavour should work well for any people-oriented business. Hathirimani also offers a number of other pointers from experience:

- The branding is consistent, everybody's Twitter handle starts off with ASTF so there's no doubt it's the company Tweeting someone. 'You have to remember the way you Tweet is like the way you send from a company email, you have to do it in a way your company expects,' he says. The business has had to remind people in the past, for example, to remember the sort of language they're using while they're Tweeting or Facebooking on the company's behalf.

- The tone can be as individual as you like but the core values have to be respected. 'Our values as a company are to be open, friendly, honest, entrepreneurial,' says Hathiramani (although if you can find a company that would disagree with those values I'd be stunned). You can find underlying issues by watching the social engagements, he says. If someone writes something that chimes badly – maybe it's abrasive, maybe it's argumentative – it could be a sign of a more general clash with corporate values.

- Take advantage, though, of someone's individuality. If the England Rugby Team turn up somewhere wearing identical suits, resident rugby fans on the staff are urged to blog about it because their passion for the sport is bound to come through and customers will find this engaging.

Hard cash

None of this would serve the company in the slightest were it not making money. This is why it has Google Analytics solidly in place on its website so it can see where the customers are coming from. More recently Adobe has come out with an analytics package.

There are useful results and figures available, which help to inform the business how it should allocate its staff's time on these networks. 'We can see that Twitter traffic doesn't generate so many appointments but it doesn't get that many clicks,' says Hathiramani; in other words few people click through to the website from Twitter compared to other electronic sources but the ones that do tend to make an appointment and/or order some clothes. So for this business it's a good way of attracting new prospects, not because they click in droves but because they tend to be more committed once they've clicked.

Like a lot of correspondents in this book, ASTF is keen to grow its business through social media but is aware that it's not possible to find out where every customer has come from. If you make an appointment on the website you're asked where you found out about the company and about 30% of people actually answer, which is a higher ratio than many manage but it's still a minority. 'Sometimes it's not black and white; you know anecdotally that some people will have seen [your Facebook or Twitter] and others will see you two or three times and buy more.' So working out the value of a Tweet in terms of what it costs and what it pays is a far from exact science. Hathiramani's answer is to look at the overall business and see how it's growing – the rest, how it would have grown without these engagements, is pretty much speculation. Facebook, while this book was being written, was getting the company about two appointments a week out of 120–130, he says, but this is only the people who have confirmed that they came through that channel. Others will have seen the page, the Tweets, maybe heard from a friend, or seen a promotion in a newspaper.

Loyalty points: another social idea

One very social way of getting more people into your virtual shop is to get existing customers to recruit them. This is part of ASTF's loyalty scheme. It works on the amount of money someone spends, like any other loyalty idea, but it also operates on referrals.

Co-founder David Hathiramani doesn't disclose figures but confirms that a lot of the company's new business comes from this scheme. It doesn't cost any more than the advertising that has been abandoned in its favour.

'Instead of spending it on Google AdWords spend it on customers,' he says. 'It makes us feel much better, it gets more product out there and it kind of makes the customers feel good, we hope, as well.' It does if they get 3000 points and a new tailored shirt for nothing, for example.

This means bloggers as well as individuals with one-to-one emails end up promoting the company, and of course the business is happy with that. It's also keen to get people to disclose that they have an interest in click-throughs – social media is all about full disclosure when done well.

There is an argument that says this looks a bit cynical – instead of a reduction as you might get in a clothes shop, you get a voucher off but only if you recruit someone throwing more money at the business. In the same way that Naked Wines (see Chapter 1) offers money back on the next purchase instead of an immediate discount, ASTF adds it up as loyalty points and scores a lot of new business in the process.

What would potentially have been missing is the pampering element, the personal service I discussed above. Hathiramani is clear that this needs to be substituted somehow and to an extent this is achieved by having all of the style advisors from the branches on the blog and on Twitter. 'It goes out to all our customers and makes us seem friendly and approachable,' he believes. 'It's part of our personality and we try and get the individuals who will actually be serving you to do it, so you get a first hand feeling of what it would be like to come in for an appointment.'

For all that, it's different. If you want wood panelling, fussing around, and all that goes with a traditional suit fitting you're still better off with a traditional tailor. This 'social' version is a modern riff; others are adopting it with either more or less electronic interaction (another one I know reasonably well, King and Allen, won't take self-measurements but sends e-newsletters and runs e-competitions and engages on Twitter – you pay your money . . .)

Both have engaged using the social media, and neither goes for the hard sell. Both have done well through the social media.

Dell

A substantially larger concern using social media extensively is Dell. It's old news by now but it's still worth revisiting that company's big impact on new customers who discovered an element of the company of which they had been unaware, and they discovered it through Twitter.

Essentially, in 2009 not everybody knew that Dell Computer was a business that would sell its computers cheaply when it was either about to redesign the whole range or upgrade them. In practical terms this means that the appearance might change but you have a perfectly workable computer, or that a more powerful version is about to become available. If your computing needs are comparatively light then you might find that the version the company has been selling happily enough for the previous three years is perfectly adequate for your needs.

Hence the refurbished store on the Dell website. People weren't as aware of it as the company wanted, so in 2007 it set about engaging with Twitter users about how they could be missing bargains. By the end of 2008 it had sold $1m in computers which it attributed directly to this feed, and on 11 June 2009 it blogged that it had reached the $2m mark. These were all sales which were tracked back to the idea of not only promoting directly through Twitter but through answering questions as well. The result was not only the $2m sales through the outlet store but a further $1m in sales to people who came in through the store then found something they'd rather have elsewhere in the store. 'I started tweeting more regularly and doing more Twitter-exclusive offers, which created more buzz and helped us to grow our follower base (we're now over 600,000). Our followers responded by re-tweeting @DellOutlet messages to their followers, and our numbers rose even more,' says the 11 June 2009 entry on the blog.

A tiny minority of readers will be able to match those sorts of numbers, and of course these figures were backed by a brand which had already been massive since the 1980s. It's a good illustration of how social media were turned to solid cash by one particular corporation when still relatively new. Dell still uses social media of course – and it's in the newer areas where there are lessons to be learned.

Public sector

Dell's Rishi Dave, executive director of online marketing, works with the public sector and large enterprise business units at the company. It's immediately obvious that social networking is maturing, because it's so often categorized as something consumers do but to which public sector and larger enterprise are less suited. Clearly if Dell has seen an opportunity this is changing. In terms of responsibility, Dave takes the social media engagement and the Dell.com engagements.

The first thing that has to be done on this scale is to make it coherent and as in other examples throughout this book, to achieve some sort of coherent corporate voice. Dell, remember, is a computer company and so employs a great many technophiles. 'What we found was that we had many employees who wanted to communicate in this way with customers, through social media' says Dave. A lot of them were a little afraid to go ahead because they didn't know whether they'd get into trouble, whether they needed permissions and so on.'

The answer for this larger corporation was to invest heavily in social media training. This means not only training people in terms of guidelines and what they may or may not say but also on how to use the different social media channels.

Select your trainer

One of the major issues with social media and social commerce, and certainly something that's cropped up since the publication of my first book, is that everybody who wants to describe themselves as a social media 'expert' or 'trainer' automatically considers themselves a qualified guru. Many have excellent insights to offer.

There is also the chancer – in any industry they crop up, but they're relatively easy to spot (my own rule is that anyone who has to tell you they're a guru probably isn't, and anyone whose Twitter profile says they're a thought leader but has ten followers is likewise either very new to the network or not to be taken all that seriously).

If, like Dell, your business needs extra training or input, then it's important to get the right person or company doing it. I'd suggest the following as guidelines:

- Sort out an objective and a brief.
  I was once asked, following the first book (which focused on small business and owner/managers), to speak to a group of 100 people in another country. I was very flattered, and accepted. I did some publicity at the host's request including some radio spots and TV spots in which I mentioned that small businesses would be welcome. Over 100 people arrived, they seemed pleased enough and then I spoke to the hosts – they were perfectly happy, particularly since (they then told me) so many bankers and local politicians had come along. OK, the host was happy but I wouldn't have delivered a small biz presentation if I'd known who'd booked and you don't want the wrong person with the wrong presentation turning up for your event either.

- Ask who else they've trained.
  Listen in particular for any mention of clients your size and with similar needs and wants. Someone might be brilliant at helping people with social media needs in the financial services sector but that's not going to help if you're in, say, the building trade.
- Ask for references.
  If they're a new trainer then don't be put off, everyone has to start sometime, but if they're reluctant to confirm this then beware – they should ideally be as up front as possible.
- Make sure they're training at the right level.
  If you're just starting in social media your needs will be very different from a company which has been using the networks for a couple of years.
- Always sanity check the price against what others are offering.
  If it sounds too good to be true . . . you know the rest.

Dell found that once it had done the training and effectively granted permission for its colleagues and employees to take part in social media it had a very motivated workforce worldwide. People were suddenly promoting the company to customers in a way they had not done before, and in ways the company hadn't expected. 'Training is an incredible component, and you also have to provide the right tools across the company,' says Dave. 'So the right listening tools – we use Salesforce.com and Radian 6.'

These are sophisticated, paid-for tracking tools for social media engagement and results; less expensive options are discussed in Chapter 8. It's essential to have something more sophisticated as a company's needs grow; these tools listen to and evaluate the business's social engagement worldwide. The company has a centralized social media command contro which monitors some 25,000 Dell mentions a day across the world, identifying opportunities, noting when positive comments are going viral and when something needs monitoring or a response.

Related to this is a centralized social media team for the worldwide business, which picks the right tools for the team overall. On this scale a business needs a governance structure about how the various properties and stakeholders interact with each other as well, so that the individual interactions at the edge of the corporation are managed and governed centrally.

Results

Once again the engagement – and you can imagine on this scale that it has required substantial budget and commitment – has to be evaluated. And as we get further away from 2009 the idea that 'this once made the company $3m' is going to be less and less of a convincing answer.

The company still measures exactly how much revenue it drives through Twitter, unlike a number of smaller businesses; this is because it can track a customer's journey through the different channels more effectively than the micro business because, frankly, it can throw money at the process. It has a social outreach team and processes which track how the business turns a detractor into an advocate, and is very conservative with its figures so that they don't get exaggerated.

This is powerful marketing information. On the business-to-business side it can be easier as the communities of customers are tighter-knit so it's easier to get to know who is buying from you. Critical customers can be identified so the company knows when it is being evaluated for a major purchase and can push them further along the sales cycle. The pattern of sale is different in that the larger business-to-business customer will typically have a longer cycle, Dave confirms, though, that the major, major driver behind the social media engagement is bringing up the bottom line sales figures.

The aim of this chapter has been to tell you something about approaching complete strangers to turn them into customers by going through the social networks. We've looked at some strategies which haven't worked in the past and established, I hope, that the sell-sell-sell approach is unlikely to produce many results beyond a group of aggrieved customers. We've seen that some of the oldest mistakes in the world have resurfaced as people have hijacked inappropriate Twitter conversations to push their own agendas and promptly fallen flat on their faces.

Then we checked over the more positive side of what's achievable, and the answer was: a very great deal. You can find new customers. You can get your customers to find new customers – come on, a referral scheme is hardly unique to social media or the Internet, but you can do it a lot more easily than you could before we all went technologized. As your business grows and gets more sophisticated it's possible to track this stuff even more thoroughly than you did before with tools that become more affordable – and the beauty of the Internet is that the thing can scale worldwide as your business develops. I'd say this globalization was relatively painless but I'm worried someone in technical support for one of the corporates would actually murder me.

Action points

- Ask yourself about your existing customers. Remember A Suit That Fits started marketing to customers who were like the management and therefore of that generation which would be on Facebook a lot.

- Look through anything visual you've prepared for your website that didn't quite work out: it might well do OK for a Twitter post, where people's expectations are for something rougher and readier.

- Take advantage of your employees' personalities, no matter how big or small the company. Remember that both A Suit That Fits and Dell found their employees willing to share their interests and engage with their customers through the social networks: you'd have a hard job finding two companies sharing less in common in terms of scale but this willingness to engage was common.

- Reward customers for recruiting each other. This has been the richest strand of new business for A Suit That Fits, which rarely appears to offer actual discounts on its site and doesn't pay for Google Adwords, spending the money on its customers instead. The result is a motivated and recruitment-hungry customer base.

- Be prepared to spend something on training. It may not be huge but it can pay back quickly, even if only because your colleagues will feel confident in taking part.

- Like Dell, try to track where people are in the sales cycle. This can seem like hard work at first but in many businesses it's nothing you won't already be doing by tracking emails and calls.

4 SUBTLE SELLING

Hey you – want to buy a book on social commerce???

Until you bought this volume the answer to that would probably have been 'yes' for most readers, hence the fact that you have this copy in your hand. Even so, if a shop owner or marketing email had put the question in those exact terms I'll bet you'd have said 'no thanks.' You'd have backed away, probably nervously, hoping the speaker would go somewhere else, no matter how much you wanted the actual book.

This is what a lot of people do in social commerce and media and it's how a lot of sales fall apart. They pressurize, they do the hard sell, they tell you that you can't cope without whatever they happen to be offering and they do it with tacky marketing language.

This chapter is for people who want to avoid that. It's about engaging with people with a view to making more profit of course – if we weren't doing something about that then why bother – but doing so in a non-aggressive manner, engaging rather than flogging. Anybody who opens up any social commerce or social media channel needs to understand that not everybody who fetches up will be interested in buying something – but that's not unique to social media. Anybody who opens a shop should be aware that not everybody who walks in is going to spend money. But they're probably interested in what you sell in the shop, so you can have a conversation and they may come back another time.

It's actually quite a good analogy. If you go to a shop to browse you need to be comfortable whether you're going to open your wallet or purse or not. If you go in intending to spend hundreds, you may not do so if you see the staff treating another customer badly because they've realized there isn't going to be a purchase – the bad feeling will rub off on the spenders.

The opposite is true as well. If you walk past a restaurant and everyone's obviously having a good time with smiling staff, you might walk into that one and take a table even if you hadn't intended to. If you'd heard a bit of buzz about it, so much the better. That's what this chapter is about: generating sales without getting too salesy, using social media to seed an environment in which people are going to want to spend their money with you.

In this chapter you will:

- Ditch the overt sales approach – it very rarely works in a context in which people are expecting a conversation

- Look at how your customers and prospects behave online already and how they're likely to appreciate being engaged

- Find good examples of engagements and bad ones and keep it relevant

- Use a non-salesy sales pitch to encourage sales

- Take a realistic look at how the indirect approach is actually affecting your financial performance, and allocate resources to suit it.

Selling for England

The first thing to do is to abandon any idea of selling actively. Let me rephrase that. The first thing to do is to abandon the idea of overt selling. By all means publicize the odd Twitter offer; telling people they're getting something in return for following you on a particular network is of course good practice, but this is like the start of a relationship. If it becomes apparent that you're not going anywhere more interesting with it, people will withdraw their interest when there are no freebies on offer (although do have a look at Chapter 9 on the judicious use of these freebies).

Let's take a few examples from real life. In the last few weeks at the time of writing I've seen my own Twitter stream cluttered with retweets from people wanting to win the following:

- A Tissot watch

- An HTC phone

- Several iPads

And all you had to do was to retweet – in other words repeat – what someone had said, usually a marketing message of some sort. Literally, someone wanting new followers on Twitter would put a note up saying 'Follow me and RT this message to win an iPad!'

Of course they get followers in the shorter term and of course the winner's going to be happy when the product actually arrives. But have a look at the message again: 'Follow me and RT this message to win an iPad!' It tells us two things:

1. The person or company wants more followers

2. He or she or it will spend £400-odd on a prize in order to get them.

It doesn't tell the reader why they might want to follow except the general desire to win something. If the company name isn't well known it doesn't tell me what it does, it doesn't tell me why I might be interested. Which is a shame because for all I know my life might be significantly better with that company involved. Most of the entrants will never know because once the promotion is over they're not going to give it another thought. In other words there has been no useful objective served, it's highly unlikely that even the winners would stay in touch. Think about spending your time that way – why would you?

I should stress that the companies manufacturing the products themselves weren't responsible in any of the cases, Apple rarely gives away iPads, for example. The messages had a complete lack of imagination – just repeating something is going to elicit one of two reactions from readers: one, they hope they win, so they retweet the message and forget all about it, or two, they get annoyed that their Twitter stream is clogged with retweets of a marketing message in which they're not interested.

Another company I'm not going to name came closer to getting it right. It was a company that sold something to do with mobile phones, so when they gave away some Bluetooth headsets from a sponsoring partner you could at least see where they were going with it, and they used a quiz format so that nobody ended up bored with the contest.

Unfortunately when the prizes arrived there was a request for a photo of the winner using their headset, with a view to displaying the pictures on Twitter and on the company's website. No such request had been made when people entered the competition so this contest had the opposite problem – it engaged people OK, then it tried to re-engage them and keep it going in an intrusive manner. The intentions were obviously fine but the execution was clumsy.

The relevant approach

Before this all gets too negative let's have a look at some positive examples. These giveaways are both utterly real but to me they're far ahead of the examples in the main text.

Elsewhere in this book there's an interview with Naked Wines. In February 2011 there was a competition on this site run by one of the small vineyards that supplies the company. It was an Italian vineyard and the prize was an expenses-paid trip over to see how the wine was made, a weekend staying there with your partner. Rather than just put up a bland message entrants had to put up a message to their loved one, and the wine maker himself decided on the winner, non-negotiable.

So he'd picked up on the fact that the followers would be interested in wine. He'd picked up that their partners would be delighted to have a message written somewhere – he hadn't researched it but it was a reasonable guess. Obviously he understood that the entire universe is interested in a free holiday if it's any good. He'd got people focusing on something other than mindless retweeting.

Granted I didn't win when clearly I should have – but the principle is very clear; people were asked to engage, think a bit, have some fun, and maybe even make their partner a little happier. It may not be to your taste but the idea of a romantic break in an Italian vineyard was closely related to the clients.

Likewise men's toiletry company Bulldog ran a competition across Twitter; it was during the football season, the product is clearly masculine, and the company's name is 'bulldog,' so it asked male followers to come up with names for canine football teams. Rather than mindless repetition of hashtagged marketing messages people had a laugh, thought of some daft names like 'Liverpoodle' and a handful won some moisturiser they could have bought for under a fiver in a supermarket. The prize and its low value wasn't the point: the idea was to have some fun and establish the company as a good one to follow for entertainment as well as information. It wasn't mindless repetition so nobody got annoyed with the hashtag.

Note the way both organizations had taken account of the likely interests and mindsets of their customers and prospects, and ensured there was a bit of targeting going on. It also helps that the companies or individuals involved were giving something of their core product away. If the prizes were any good and people started talking about them online there could only be positive consequences.

Facebook: A great venue for engagement

If Twitter is a good place to engage then Facebook, where people can exchange ideas and you can see a threaded conversation, is even better. It's on Facebook that Penderyn, the Welsh Whisky company, interacts with a lot of people interested in the brand and the world of malt whiskies in general. It does so in such a way that it encourages more people to try the brand but it never says anything as blatant as 'go and try our product' or 'there's a fiver off in the supermarkets.'

Facebook itself asks people not to register when they are under 13; Penderyn has gone further both in this and on its own website in ensuring people have to confirm they are over 18 – along with all companies selling alcohol their concern is to carry out their business legally and responsibly.

Before the company became involved a number of people who liked the whisky started putting together what was then called a 'fan page' and would now be called simply a Facebook page. They liked swapping ideas about whiskies they'd enjoyed and some were diehard Penderyn fans, not only because of the drink but because of its novelty value as the only Welsh single malt. Members of staff heard what was going on and started to join the Facebook fan page when there were around 150 members. Stephen Davies, managing director, explains that the numbers started to ramp up quite quickly with no official promotion from the company. 'Then the organizer quickly contacted us and said look, this is starting to build a little bit, do you guys want to be the administrators of the site? We thought it was a good idea and here we are over two and a half years later and we've got nearly 4000 members.'

It was the company's PR person and non-executive director Joshua Van Raalte who realized the social media element had some serious potential benefit. This led to Davies allocating some of his time to becoming an administrator of the page and asking his commercial director to do the same, and they have an external person keeping an eye on it when they are doing other things. Planning and structuring was very important once it had been taken in-house. 'We've actually got a plan now where we all have a slot over the next few months to contribute,' explains Davies. Note the planning in advance; if a business wants Facebook to deliver customers it can't be done 'when people have a minute' because they never get one. The time taken in engaging with people on the social media needs to be costed and factored in to a business plan.

What's on the page

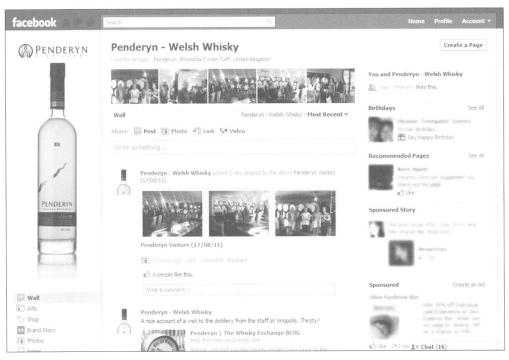

Source: www.facebook.com/penderyn page used with permission of Agency Brazil. Facebook and the Facebook logo are trademarks of Facebook, Inc.

The actual content can depend a lot on what the company is doing at a particular time. In 2011 Davies sent messages and photos from a whisky show on Lake Lucerne, for example. 'It was interesting to be in a show in Switzerland, talking to people who we'd also been talking to on Facebook,' he says. 'So we kind of felt we were reaching people who were keen on the brand, who were followers of the brand and it's their opportunity to feed into us what they think and a great opportunity for us to bounce ideas out.' As a very small business, the company enjoys the chance to connect with people who are actually drinking its product.

Nonetheless this has to connect to the bottom line somehow. Surely the idea is to make money, otherwise why bother? This works in two ways. First there is branding and brand loyalty as well as encouraging people to come to the visitor centre. The visitor centre manager posts to the Facebook page. 'Keith will regularly post pictures of people who are visiting the distillery,' explains Davies. 'When the whisky writer Jim Murray came here, he did an impromptu tasting on Penderyn 41 and that's posted on Facebook and things like that are very interesting for people to see.'

'So it's a way of raising the profile of the visitor centre and hopefully persuading people to come and visit us. Then when people visit, we post their pictures on Facebook – with their permission of course – and they then become followers.' The overall effect is a sort of drip-fed encouragement of brand loyalty among people who may previously only have been casual customers. People who don't get to the visitor centre get a sense of some sort of buzz – visitors are welcomed with their pictures on the Facebook page as well as welcomed in person.

The second way the company makes something from social media is to highlight the brand whenever it can. A lot of this is in answering questions. People read about the whisky and ask 'I'm in Adelaide, Australia, where can I get a bottle of Penderyn?'

Go to the market, don't expect it to come to you

The Penderyn example highlights an old truism in the retail trade: people will never do what you want them to. If, as happens sometimes, someone asks where they can get a bottle of the whisky in (for example) Australia then there's actually nothing to stop them having a look at the website and finding out.

The customers elect not to.

There could be a number of reasons. The site is clear enough so it's not an alienation thing. It's easy to navigate so it's not that. It seems simply to be that if people have the choice they'd rather stay on Facebook where they know they're going to get a bit of a chat and find some more like-minded people.

A good lesson for other businesses on Facebook is not to try to take the market away from where it likes to play. Facebook actually gives a lot of people a digital 'home' – that's where you need to make the sale.

Facebook-centricity has applied to Penderyn's blog too. 'We started a blog on the website, but we quickly realised that any blogging that we were going to do was better done through Facebook and Twitter,' says Davies, because people gravitate towards these places rather than a business's own website.

You'll notice the mention of Twitter as well as Facebook just now. The company is more active on Facebook than Twitter but Davies and his staff are aware of the importance of covering both; in simple commercial terms it's a matter of making sure they go wherever the customer wants to find them online. The days when you could put a virtual shop front up and hope people came to you aren't actually dead – many companies sell successfully from their own website – but if you're small it's a lot simpler to go to where the customer is already spending most of their day.

Both networks end up with a lot more discussion and engagement than overt selling. 'It's very much about finding out about the brand and talking about the interesting aspect, that naturally sells the product,' says Davies. 'I think malt Whisky drinkers are people who are naturally inquisitive, they want to find out, they want to be able to talk to their friends about different brands and different aspects of the brands that they like and so it's very much a discussion based thing.' This is an important point because it demonstrates an understanding of the customer, which enables the company to address them appropriately.

Soft sell

There's a link on the Facebook page to the company's online store and it hardly gets mentioned by the staff themselves, almost as if the idea of bringing up sales will put people off. 'If you look at the day to day things that are posted, they tend to be about the tasting and about the appearances of the brand in different places. We don't see it as a mechanism to really sell hard, but to build a fan base and to build knowledge about the brand,' says Davies.

So no overt selling, as has been established already. There is an underlying philosophy in this and many of the other businesses selling successfully through the social networks that the sale is a relatively small part of the transaction.

Tracking sales: the impossible task

This could be just as well because telling whether a particular sale came from the company's online interaction is very tricky. The drinks industry has a particular feature: UK licensing laws mean they may not sell overseas through the Internet. This means that when that person asks where they can buy a bottle in Adelaide, there is no way of telling whether any of the Adelaide sales were made as a result of that exchange. Likewise people buying a bottle in Sainsbury's may have been influenced by a friendly exchange with the business on Twitter but there is absolutely no way anybody could say for certain.

This is among the reasons Penderyn in particular sees the networks as a place for branding, and this is something other businesses would do well to consider. Davies comments: 'I think you can say with some degree of confidence that by linking up with people on social media, it is helping the brand to be established, spreading the word. Because the way our brand has always grown has been by personal contacts in the first instance and by people discovering it and then telling their friends. It's an extension of that as far as I'm concerned.'

So there is no actual measurement as to how the social media is affecting solid sales? 'We grew sales, probably not far off 30% last year and yes, you can't actually say that a percentage of that is down to social media, but it's a very important part of the marketing mix for us,' says Davies.

Changing mix

Other social networks are becoming established and the company is aware they could become important; it has noted people uploading pictures of their visitor centre tours and indeed their bottles on Flickr and, as in the Facebook example, this helps the branding.

Taking feedback seriously is also less expensive on Facebook than it might be elsewhere. People visiting the visitor centre had been disappointed not to see the company doing its own maltings, which is a process that happens at the Brains Brewery, so this was taken on board and made clearer on the website to manage expectations.

Appropriacy

Just because something can be done doesn't mean it should, of course. Even if it looks harmless enough.

Whisky, and particularly fine single malt, isn't cheap and in terms of demographics it tends not to attract very young adults. This doesn't put Penderyn off being as diligent as it can about just how the brand is promoted. Davies mentions a Welsh festival recently in which someone dressed as a comedic dragon was seen cavorting – not drunkenly or harmfully – around the branding. This had made its way to the company's YouTube channel but was subsequently taken down, not because the person dressed as the mascot had done anything untoward or inappropriate but because it was an image that might appeal to children and Penderyn is very conscious of keeping any childhood associations away from the brand. The chances of any harm being done are phenomenally small but Davies is adamant – if a child is going be able to find a video on YouTube that brings the world of whisky to them in a child-like manner then it comes down.

Company strategy

Another way in which Penderyn has used the social networks is to find out what the customer would like in terms of company strategy. It does this in two ways: first the more proactive, it actually asks them from time to time, and second the observational, when it watches what they are doing online and reacts accordingly.

A simple anecdote illustrates the proactive approach very straightforwardly. How would you spell whisky? There's a clue in the question of course but you'd be just as entitled to spell it whiskey, if it's Irish or American, and the original Welsh spelling from previous generations that had a whisky industry was Wysgi.

When working on the branding the company wanted to know how people wanted their tipple spelled so it did a survey. Whisky, the same as Scotch, came out top so that's what the business used – a small thing but something that made the customers feel involved nonetheless.

On a more substantial level the social media helps the company towards where it should be directing its next efforts. It didn't have many sales in the US while this book was being researched but that's where a quarter of its Facebook members are based. Opportunities for them to actually taste were relatively few, which will hamper the brand's growth to an extent, but there's definite early interest. So the company knows that if it wants to try marketing in America then there is already a solid bedrock of interest. Compare this to the cost of test marketing that would have been necessary otherwise and you can see that social media has given the business an insight into a new market which otherwise could have proven very expensive indeed.

Bluebeards ahoy: Conversing with partners

Other companies have less internationalism in their ambitions but still find the social media work well for them. It's not always about finding new consumers, although expanding the ability to trade is still important.

Nick Gibbens is online marketing and PR manager for The Bluebeards' Revenge – not a pirate company or anything to do with it but a manufacturer of quality shaving creams and soothing gels for hirsute men. It's self-evident that some men have heavier beard growth than others and the claim of Bluebeards' Revenge is that it actually inhibits regrowth so five o'clock shadow takes a lot longer to reappear every day.

His perception of his task is that he has to maintain the brand and yes, the company gets a number of sales from Twitter and a handful from Facebook. Like Penderyn, however, the team regards its job as branding rather than overt selling. An interesting wrinkle from The Bluebeards' point of view is that not only does it use the networks to talk to its customers, existing and potential, but also to trade partners. 'We use Twitter and Facebook to find new stockists,' says Gibbens. 'It's a great communication tool where we can engage with potential stockists and build relationships. It also allows us to distribute all the press coverage we generate, which stockists see, thus providing a great showcase for our brand and its growing popularity in the press.' Targeted correctly at the right stockists who are online and on the networks this coverage becomes a powerful tool in persuading people to take the product on.

Getting that coverage in the first place is also facilitated by the social networks, he explains. 'Twitter is also a great tool for developing press/media contacts. By simply using hash tags we can communicate with journalists who are looking for prizes and so on.'

Of course the consumers like to talk directly as well. This is why the company is happy to talk about shaving issues and male skin care in general as well as its own products. It's aware that the stockists and potential stockists can see the company engaging with and talking directly to the people who form their customer base. There is no hard sell, just engagement in creating a buzz around the brand, says Gibbens: the hard sell simply doesn't work, particularly in an area where people feel they are on 'their' computer or phone, regardless of whether they're actually using a network owned by someone else.

The company has found it easy to engage with companies and partners who want prizes which help it to increase its brand awareness and the odd giveaway on one of the social networks helps establish that. Partners the company has contacted on the social networks have included Truelad, Men's Health, GroomedGeezer, and FinerCut. Gibbens adds that the company finds it easy on Twitter to transcend a few boundaries.

The two companies interviewed in this chapter were of course well suited to the social media/social commerce approach. As Davies comments, whisky drinkers like to discuss their dram of choice (if you're allowed to use that Scottish word about something from Wales!) – it's by nature a social activity and that market will enjoy taking part.

There are learnings of course, and one of those is always to prepare and plan. Penderyn's Davies mentions that a blogger arrived at his office one day hoping for an interview, carrying a video camera. He was wearing the corporate t-shirt so he agreed but had to deal with an important call first; it took longer than expected and although there is no trace of impatience in his voice on the video he feels he looks tired and a little unfocused.

I'm a media trainer as well as journalist and author and a big no-no if you're responsible for a brand is a genuinely off-the-cuff interview. Davies' interview is actually fine, I've watched it, but he'd clearly have been happier if it had been done another way – preparation would have made a difference.

If readers took only one thing away from this chapter, though, it would be the point from which we started that new customers need to be engaged, wooed, in fact anything but sold to very overtly. People run some way from the hard sell and if it's on the Internet it's very easy to switch off or to click on something else.

Social media can work and have worked extremely well for the Penderyn brand, and indeed Davies believes it's great for a brand which is at the beginning of its lifecycle. On hearing about other companies doing less well with social media engagements – at the time of our meeting there were reports around about one high profile company investing a lot and not getting any return from its latest social media campaign – Davies in fact reflected that his task had been to build brand awareness rather than build sales directly (although any MD of a company with a premium-priced brand that put 30% of sales on during a particularly nasty recession should be feeling relatively pleased with that side of the business too).

Both interviewees agreed that the hard sell was out and communication was in. It's important, too, to be realistic about the level of commitment an engagement in this way is going to take up. Take the Penderyn example: as was established earlier, what started as a fan page run by someone outside of the company now takes up time from three people including the MD, the commercial manager, and one external person.

It also offers some substantial opportunities, though, and the meetings with followers in Lucerne illustrate that the chance to build brand loyalty is very real if the idea is resourced well enough.

Action points

There are a number of things people could do with their own business, whether it's something that attracts an obviously social customer base or not:

- Look at any social media promotions you may be planning. If they consist only of getting people to repeat your tag line, take them out and shoot them – nobody's going to enjoy them.

- If you can make them appealing and align them to your brand as in the first shaving company example, which took advantage of the masculine customer base, the canine name, and everybody's sense of humour, so much the better.

- Penderyn has a rough plan of what's going to go into its Facebook page covering quite some time in advance. Do the same, and cost the time – make sure it's going to be worth it.

- Go to the market – don't expect it to turn up on your website after reading a pleasant piece on Facebook.

- Ditch any hard sell tactics as soon as you think of them. Listen as well as talk to your Facebook members and other social media followers and reply to their questions as well as offer promotions.

- Consider your objectives and whether you can measure your success directly. Remember the Penderyn example; the company has no way of knowing whether a particular sale is going to be part of its social media engagement. Put metrics in place which will tell you how your engagement is performing.

- Remember other people may be watching – possible trade partners, for example. They will be very interested to see how you go about generating demand for your goods or services and may end up making a decision on working with you as a result. You're always on show!

5 CUSTOMERS AND BEYOND – THE DIFFERENT COMMUNITIES YOU CAN TALK TO

So far in this book we have looked at taking advantage of the direct communication with customers that's possible with the electronic media. We've established that whole new business models are possible, whether you regard them as entirely new innovations or extensions of older ideas like the co-operative movement. (Note: an author will always and without fail tell you he's seen a business model before. It's what we do.)

In this chapter we're going to look at some of the other innovations the electronic media are facilitating. First we'll be going beyond the standard text and picture stuff that's on everybody's Twitter stream and using a bit of innovation to make it really immersive – second we'll be looking at communities who may not be trading partners directly but who can make a powerful difference to your company – finding investors, finding employees. We'll also have a look beyond the computer-based social media and have a play with the fact that people use more than one device.

First we'll look at talking to your potential workforce. There will also be a glance at a brewery which used social media to raise capital, just as this book was going to press. Finally – and I'm not making this up – it'll be back to the customer with a look at making a space monkey dance by singing to your phone. I have not been taking drugs.

In this chapter, then, you should pick up the following:

- A look at the different communities with whom you can engage

- Taking people by surprise

- Raising funds through social media

- Working with third parties

- A look at different ways in which clients can be made to engage beyond straight text – so games, videos, handsets.

Social media for explaining stuff

I present at several social media conferences and seminars for business. For my first year one of my main theories was that as well as some excellent contacts and means of offering expertise and support to customers, there were – from the business point of view – some complete time wasters. People who only wanted to play games, chat to friends, whatever else they might want to do. Not that there's anything wrong with playing games and hanging out with your friends, far from it. For businesses, though, these activities had nothing going for them unless you were in the area of games development.

I've had to moderate my view slightly. Sorry, did I say slightly? Let's modify that and say that the activities of Marriott Hotels worldwide and its recruitment efforts, which involve explaining its business in some depth through a Facebook game, have forced me to change my views totally.

There's a whole book to be written on gamification (he hinted). This is the process by which the trappings of games – earning badges and so forth – are added to non-game applications. So you can now get badges from Google for reading news stories on its site, for example. The idea is to take advantage of the fact that the human psyche is designed to rather enjoy games so if you can persuade your brain that you're playing while you're actually working, it'll work a bit harder. The same principle applies to FourSquare, which is certainly a loyalty scheme but which more or less turns planet Earth into a game location and offers points or badges when you reach certain levels, locations, branches of Tesco.

With that in mind we're going to look at the Marriott Hotel in Mumbai, India, and how the company has added an entirely new dimension to its recruitment process through social media.

The location is actually quite important. Dubai has particular social conditions. Tourists who go there are often fabulously rich and people who live nearby aren't. This is what Dr David Kippen, head of social media engagement agency Evviva in Los Angeles, came across when he visited the premises.

He and his agency had been approached by the company to build its brand in China and India. Marriott was aware that its brand was understood primarily by Western travellers; it would be wrong to say it wasn't known elsewhere but it wasn't as strong as the company needed it to be. 'We did focus groups, but we also spent a lot of time doing ethnography, going down into the heart of the house, dining with the staff, really trying to walk around and to the extent that you can, as an outsider, walk a mile in the shoes of the people we were learning about,' he explains. He was staying at the JW Hotel in Mumbai. The location was spectacular, the U-shaped building allowed for a beach view from just about every room. So he asked the workers how they had come to find the place and to find out about the jobs they now occupied. They said, almost universally, that they had come to Mumbai having lived in a small village in order to better themselves. They added that they hadn't known many people so they had ended up spending a lot of time on their computers or phones building up their social networks.

They were on Bebo (although this has faded), foreign language network Orkut, and of course Facebook. The next question was how long they spent doing this networking and the answer would be that they'd go to a Cybercafe and keep on the networks for hours. 'I'd say well come on guys, you can't convince me that you're actually, actively networking for six or eight hours a day,' says Dr Kippen. 'What else are you doing? And they'd sheepishly admit to well, you know, I also like to play social games.' Crucially he now had an idea of where his target client group actually was with its online social interactions. It is vital, particularly if you want people to understand concepts which are new, to take the information to them wherever they are already comfortable rather than try to push them onto your own preferred platform.

He made a mental note of all of this and another strand of how this social network readiness could be useful occurred to him while he was in the hotel's lounge. 'I noticed that there were a group of people on the beach looking up at the hotel,' he explains. He noticed one of the employees (or 'associates' to use Marriott's own terminology) from his focus group so he asked her what these people were actually doing. 'She said, dismissively, but not unkindly, oh they're just curious about what goes on here. They have no idea.'

This, he realized, was inevitable. The local community had no conception of going on holiday to a hotel and having a waiter bring you a drink, having someone else clean your room and make your bed, having a conference hall for corporate events. It wasn't part of their world, without any patronization intended there was just about no way they could be expected to understand what was going on. 'I decided to go out and have a look and see the hotel as they saw it, and it was a real eye opener,' he says. 'It had past my attention because of how common it is in emerging markets, that when I came in the front of the hotel, I was greeted with you know, the bomb sniffing dog.' That wasn't all. He soon realized just how far apart these worlds were conceptually. Turn one way and you're in paradise. Turn the other and see the hotel from the locals' point of view and you're confronting a fortress with armed guards and a blast wall.

Dr Kippen stresses, rightly, that this doesn't reflect Marriott's view or aspiration of where it should be as a brand or as a culture. 'In every focus group I conducted, unbidden, the groups would respond back when I asked them why they liked Marriott, with what I came to learn was Mr Marriott's second rule of service and that was, take care of the associate, the associate will take care of the guests and the guests will come back.' Outside looked like a fortress because it was in an area where there had been terrorist attacks, simple as that.

He had found similar levels of cultural disparity on visiting the company's premises in Thailand, too. So he knew the people outside didn't understand what was going on inside, that they couldn't work out why someone would pay all that for a cup of tea. He knew that they were very hot on social media and that they played a lot of games.

So Evviva created a hotel game that works on Facebook. Here's a picture:

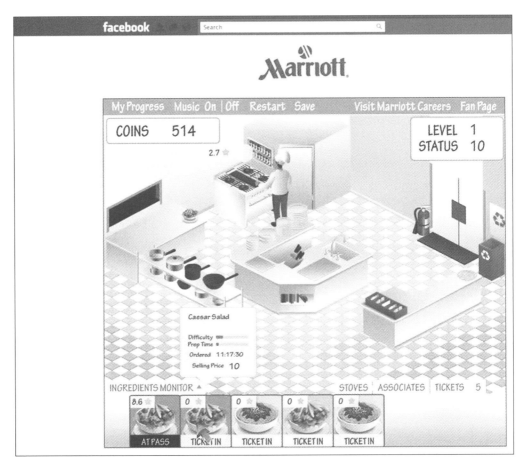

Source: www.facebook.com/marriottjobsandcareers page used with permission of Spreckly Partners Ltd. Facebook and the Facebook logo are trademarks of Facebook, Inc.

Social media agencies

It's worth stepping back at this stage and considering that Evviva was and is a very different company from Marriott, its client in this case. It's not in the catering and hospitality industry, it's not a worldwide concern (although clearly it services worldwide clients). There is a lot to be learned from how the companies made the cultures work together as a partnership – other companies looking to work with agencies might like to take note of some of the methods.

First, Evviva as an agency is very focused on clients in the service industries. Over the years it has found that's what it's good at; if a company isn't a 'people brand' then Evviva understands it's probably not the right agency to work with that company. Other organizations looking for partners would do well to look for a similar focus in the right area. Second, it takes time to understand the brand with which it is going to work. 'We say, I can't be you, but I can try to learn what interests you and probably, if I'm doing my job right, I fall in love a little bit with the work you do too,' says Dr Kippen. Many marketing agencies have a bit of a 'vanilla' approach – they say what they'll do and they do it, regardless of the client and their needs.

Kippen's words might sound like one of those platitudes a candidate from the BBC *The Apprentice* show might come out with, amounting to precious little in practical terms. In this instance it translates into a great deal of very practical measures indeed. In the Marriott engagement the company did actual cleaning tasks, visiting premises and behaving as much like hotel staff as it could. 'This is one of the more difficult things to do with clients, because often they'll have legal concerns and moral concerns about doing it, but our perfect engagement is one in which we'll work with the housekeepers to make beds for example,' says Dr Kippen. 'If we can't get behind the counter at the kitchen, we'll go down dressed as closely as we can to how staff dress, and try to sit down with people and chat over meals. We'll walk round with the gardeners and try to prune hedges if they'll let us.' Any agency putting itself forward as a potential partner is going to claim it will get to know your business. Don't be afraid to dig beyond this and find out what they mean by that; the good ones, as in this example, will tell you.

This might be appropriate for your business – if you're using an agency, are they willing to get that close to you as a client? Do you want them to?

Developing the game and monitoring the results

Marriott was unexpectedly positive about the idea of the game in the first instance and threw enough money at it so that Evviva had carte blanche to develop it. The idea was that people could enter the hotel online and find out about the tasks that had to be performed and why – just to get the feel of the inside of a hotel.

The idea that this would work chimed well with experience Dr Kippen had already gleaned working for the likes of IT companies and researching their job market. New candidates and employees might not have picked up much during their formal classes. 'I may not have learned that much from my professors, they'd say, it was my class that taught me and one of the most important things I walked away with is a great email distribution list,' he explains. 'So as we all go out on the job market, we're constantly emailing one another and saying, here's what I've found, what do you know about this company, who do you know over at that company.' This, although nobody called it that a decade or more ago, was essentially social networking so the backdrop was ready – the audience was known to be in the habit of going onto social networks; behaviours of previous generations suggested they'd welcome this sort of interaction and information through their computer screens.

Other factors were considered carefully, too. The target audience would welcome the notion of the game partly because of the brand behind it, both parties felt. 'I think people have, perhaps naively, in emerging markets, a much greater trust that big brands don't do bad things by and large,' says Kippen, although there are some pretty high profile exceptions! 'So the fact that it's endorsed by a Marriott brand, I would imagine, probably means it's just fine. I just wouldn't expect there to be a lot of scepticism about that.'

This was reinforced by the minimum amount of information the game required. People considering doing something similar need to bear in mind how many games and apps on the Facebook site insist on the player handing over their name, phone number, and inside leg measurement. This game asked no more than the client would already have made available on their Facebook page. Trust was established by these two elements.

International appeal

The game succeeded and not just in Mumbai. The themes – not knowing exactly what goes on in a hotel from the staff's point of view, and wanting a job – aren't just India-specific, they are completely international.

Kippen offers some statistics on the take-up, backed by a PR campaign drawing it to people's attention. Some of the headline numbers are:

- Game played in 101 countries within three weeks of its launch – that's 52% of the countries in the world.

- Biggest take up is in the US then the UK; after this Hungary, Brazil, France, and then Taiwan.

- Marriott careers page had 6400 fans when the game launched and within three weeks it had over 10,000.

'The question is going to be, over time, to what extent is this a brand driver, to what extent is it just about a fun and playable game and how does it play out in employment over the longer term,' says Kippen.

Over 6000 people played it within the first few weeks and all of them would have finished on a page that said 'Now try it for real' and invited them to apply. The brand is being extended and the range of people who understand the processes their new jobs will involve has expanded because social media has enabled game playing to become part of a process in which it previously had no place. It's reached out to entirely new people and is going to have a wider choice of employee as a result.

The colour of money

It should of course save the business a great deal of money. Recruitment takes a lot of time, agencies charge a lot of money, and a lot of them have a pretty scattergun approach to sending CVs out. This idea is different; it targets a specific demographic and takes the explanation of the job environment to their computers. The principle should be transferrable to any work setting – perhaps you're in catering and could have a game exploring different areas of the kitchen, or perhaps you run an editorial office and a game could explain the different parts of writing, editing, page layout, and so forth?

There are other innovative approaches to social media. Why muck about with games, you might ask – why not just ask interested people for some money? This is what one company did when it wanted £2.2m for expansion – it just told its customers it wanted some cash and they handed it over.

There are a number of ways of getting finance if you want to expand your business:

- Use your own money

- Ask the bank, but finances have been tight for years now

- Approach an external investor.

Exit point

People tend to be terrified by the idea that there should be some sort of exit point. This is the 'how I get out of this with a load more money than I started out' bit, and it's something about which people can get unduly shy.

This is possibly the most important point for investors and it's too often overlooked by people pitching for backing. Raising money socially certainly won't expose you to the same professionalism or indeed ruthlessness you would see from a venture capitalist, but your new partners – no matter how many of them there are – need to see this as a safe place for their money. They must understand how much risk they are exposed to. More importantly they must understand how and when they can get their money out, when they can sell their shares and what the plan is to make these shares grow in value.

Many people will make small investments for a bit of fun and to support a small business. But it's an investment nonetheless, and people will need to understand the implications.

Scottish microbrewery Brewdog went a step away from the third of those ideas and invited its customers and social media fans to become shareholders. It launched the promotion – called 'Equity for Punks' to go with its punk-themed packaging – first in 2009 and then repeated it in 2011 when it needed funds to build and open a second brewery. The idea was simple: after consulting with all of its legal and accounting professionals the company issued small amounts of shares to very small investors, so you could buy (for example) four shares for £85. You could buy over the Internet with no need to arrange a broker or other intermediary.

Co-founder James Watt, speaking at the launch of the second of these rounds of funding, confirmed that people would be able to trade shares after an initial period of over one year and then the business would float on the Alternative Investments Market (in other words these are legitimate, ordinary shares) but he stressed that it was the social nature of the offering that was causing the most interest. 'We think it's a totally new and innovative way of raising capital,' he said. 'People who like what we do, who drink the beers, can have an ownership stake in our business. As well as finance for the strong growth we need for the company we also get to build a culture and a community.'

What was really striking about the idea was the importance of social media in both the initial offering in 2009 and the 2011 version. 'One of the big things we learned in 2009 was the importance of that culture and community. In 2009 we had more traditional press coverage where we were able to comment on financials and statistics in more depth but that didn't really affect [the community members] very much. What really affected them was things like Facebook, like YouTube, like Vimeo.' The company told everyone about the offer on its Facebook page and Tweeted the life out of it, both as individuals and on the company's account. The result was 3000 hits on the website, 10,000 members (or fans as they were called at the time) on the Facebook page. 'We see those as the kind of people who are going to invest, the people who are online and who know and like what we're doing.'

The success of the scheme in 2011 was considerable. It raised £500K in two days – £300K of which was in the coffers by the end of the first morning of the offer. Watt believes this is a very up-to-date way of raising money from a community which is already engaged – and which, let's be honest (and this is my input, not something he says) has been watching TV shows about starting businesses and getting involved for several years by now.

This could help the businesses of a large number of readers of this book, but do have a look at the 'Diving In' chapter to see the help on offer from Crowd Cube. There will need to be professional advisors on hand of course. An accountant would have to issue the shares, the certification would need to be properly done, and it would all need to be watertight legally. You knew that. Take a look at the box on Doctor Who to see how similar ideas have gone wrong in the past.

Flashback: Doctor Who vs Scratchman

In the 1970s, the British TV show *Doctor Who* was on a high – so why, when the BBC was making movies of all its second-tier TV sitcoms, wasn't there a Doctor Who movie? The answer is that there very nearly was.

In the mid to late 1970s, the then incumbent actor, Tom Baker, and his old colleague Ian Marter, who was also a writer, decided they should set up a film. They had an idea that the Doctor should meet Scratchman – an old name for the Devil – and some animated scarecrows. The problem, as is the case with so many movie projects, was finding the finance.

They hit on a brilliant idea, so it seemed. Baker had a column in a then popular news magazine, *Reveille* – and he invited readers to send specific donations in, for which they would be allocated shares.

He has been interviewed about this many times and freely admits it was a naïve idea. After legal advice on how to turn all these fans – some of them very generous – into shareholders he conceded that the film was unlikely to be made and returned every penny. There is no question of either Baker or Marter doing anything illegal or dishonest.

It's a long time ago, possibly a more naïve time when it comes to the difficulty of setting up and funding a business. But it's a telling story about the practicalities and legalities of group funding – it needs to be watertight.

Customers: it's not just about text

Don't forget that customers can be engaged in different ways. Customers can be harnessed for inexpensive market research of course but they can also be made to interact in different ways and you can hold their attention for longer. And a more entertaining and immersive experience is likely to lead to more engagement and that's when they spend more money.

Take the Old Spice publicity campaign from 2010. Old Spice was a successful aftershave from a couple of generations ago which has made a comeback. The campaign with which the company scored such a hit was from ad agency Wieden+Kennedy. The brand hired actor Isaiah Mustafa who recorded an ordinary advert but also hundreds – literally – of personalized responses to viewers' questions. These were incorporated into YouTube videos. Of course the answers were as daft as anything and very Old Spice oriented: think of gadget website Gizmodo's question 'Dear Old Spice, will anything surpass the loofa as the predominant body wash application technology' and an answer like 'Good question, Gizmodo, my preferred method of Old Spice body wash application is a live wolverine. They are terribly unruly but their fur permits the ideal mix of lather and exfoliation. I've also found that live puffer fish and decommissioned hand grenades work' and you get the idea.

As entertainment it was great. As a personalized service, with (I stress) literally hundreds of personalized and well-scripted humorous responses, it was engagement with a previously dated brand on a scale not seen before. It's difficult to imagine it being surpassed any time soon.

Sales went up. Equally importantly for manufacturer P&G, the campaign ran in July which meant that by the time the Christmas shopping season kicked in the brand was seen as amusing and ironic as well as up to date and capable of engaging, rather than that pong your dad used to wear before blokes discovered deodorant and therefore needed more subtle scents.

This was genius and looking at the comments on YouTube it was very well received. Of course it costs a lot to put something like this on YouTube and to personalize the whole thing. But it does illustrate that different sorts of engagement are possible.

Honda gets appy

Nowadays many customers have more than one device with them. Arguably you can deal with the multi-screen customer as a community all by themselves. Whether Facebook, Twitter, Vimeo, or other network based, the participant has had one window into the social media life of the company he or she is contacting.

So what if you had an app – one of those little programs that sits on an iPhone, or Android phone, or some other mobile device, which takes advantage of the fact that most people have more than one gadget for their social interactions? This is what Honda did specifically for the launch of its Jazz car in early 2011, with a nifty little piece of entertainment that allowed a character to hop from screen to screen, device to device.

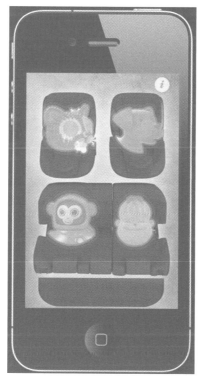

Image used with permission of Agency Brazil.

The video, also available on YouTube, used audio recognition technology to sync the app with the advert's soundtrack and allow the viewer to interact with it in real time. You were able to download and play with characters from the ad as well, such as:

- A puppy which would chase its tail in different directions when you tickled it on a touch sensitive screen

- A space monkey that would dance and throw some crazy moves (Honda said) when people sang to it on the phone

- An evolving pet with a big tail which would change species when you shook your phone

- A playable on-screen drum kit

- A plane that would lift off when you tapped its propeller.

There were others too, and you were able to collect them on your devices and then send them from your iPhone to your iPod to your iPad.

Martin Moll, Honda's head of marketing in the UK, explains that like the Marriott/Facebook example, the scheme was launched with an agency, Wieden + Kennedy, to allow people to interact with characters in an advertisement in a different way. 'We wanted to increase engagement – Honda and W+K recognized that people have a growing tendency towards consuming media across multiple screens, and this idea is in keeping with that,' he says. 'The app and advert were designed to make it challenging to capture all of the characters in one go, in order to drive people online where they could view the advert in full. Our strategy was to create engagement rather than just one-way communication and demonstrate a warm, playful nature, with the ultimate aim of entering into a two way dialogue with our audience.'

Publicizing the app was an important element of its success – no business should ever overlook the importance of the offline side of getting their engagements in front of the target customer. PR agency Agency Brazil got it mentions in blogs and other creative outlets while W + K made certain it chimed with the TV advertising as well as Honda's social video resources, where viewers could try and 'catch' the characters again.

'The campaign was successful in that the online video amassed more than 200,000 views. Honda's UK web traffic is also up 15 per cent since last year (2010), and although this is not directly attributable to the campaign, it has certainly made a strong contribution, says Moll. 'Thanks to the campaign, we've maintained significant interest in the Honda Jazz, and successfully kept a broader, younger audience engaged – an important part of our long-term strategy.'

The campaign effectively married up an objective of attracting younger people and their desire – as in the Marriott example – to do more than sit and watch an advert passively or just a text-based screen. You may find that your own business lends itself to some sort of interactive, fun app given the right agency – and do have another look at the box on finding the right agency for your business.

Action points

This chapter has been about opening up what you can do with social media and social commerce. We've looked at ways of selling which involve games and tailored video, we've looked at recruitment and raising funds by addressing the communities involved in those areas, which may not be customers at all. You could consider the following:

- Look into individualizing social contact where people aren't expecting it. The Old Spice example was spoken about for months afterwards.

- If there's something you want to explain to people – a concept, how something works – which they can't actually see, look beyond text and even beyond pictures – a Facebook game might be an excellent way of communicating.

- Look at the social media agencies with whom you are considering working. How ready are they to engage with you – do they understand your business and will they work alongside you until they do?

- Ask any social media agency wanting to work with you whether they are active in your field already. Remember they are a social media agency so there's no reason to assume they'll empathize with your business automatically.

- For funding, consider social media as an alternative means of finding backers.

- If you're going to crowd-fund an idea or an expansion, make absolutely sure you know what you're doing or that you're talking to a professional advisor who knows. You want to emulate the Brewdog boys, not the *Doctor Who* actors who found themselves sadly out of their depth.

6 BUILDING A COMMUNITY

I f there's one thing that raises my hackles in the social media world then it's the over-use of the word 'community' – says the man who's just written a chapter on some of the different ones you can address.

To me, mostly a community has active participants and if I'm identified as part of an online community I expect to be contributing to it with blog posts, looking at Facebook pages and probably contributing to them or at least chucking in the odd relevant Tweet. I expect, overall, at least to be aware I'm a member of one community or another.

Unfortunately it's a term with which we're a bit stuck, and it becomes even more nebulous when you're trying to build up your customer base. The 'community' of prospective customers is probably clear to you but they have yet to give their consent to take part in any sort of cohesive group.

So for our purposes a 'community' is a loose grouping of people and that grouping is mostly in the eye of the beholder. The job seekers' community might become your target, or the wine buff community, or just about any other sort of community – it doesn't mean they know each other or that they identify themselves as any sort of distinct bunch of people.

It's a useful concept in marketing terms. It means you can stratify your approach and start to regard clients and prospects as a cohesive bunch of people. And then turn them into regular customers and hopefully into advocates for your brand.

In this chapter you will:

● Learn to think about and address 'communities' and what this actually means in practical terms

● Select the right social media to address these communities and harness their online behaviours accordingly

● Turn them from passive recipients of social media into more active members and hopefully brand advocates

- Learn to take the 'world wide' bit out of 'world wide web' and make it local again

- Build local customer communities

- Make people feel involved and therefore motivated to come back

- Select the right social media to address those people and get them addressing each other

- Make your service feel completely personalized.

So, what sort of communities do your customers belong to? No, I'm not talking about basic demographics – white, black, Asian, male, female; these will all help you target the right people to an extent but there's more. Age groups will also help you target people and nobody is saying you should ever lose sight of those marketing basics – they're still important.

The great advantage of online communities is that since people log on in their hundreds of thousands if not millions, you can be really granular about who you're targeting. Never mind looking at the male, middle-aged community; how about the male middle-aged community which is interested in moisturiser, cologne, and other personal care products but which doesn't want to go to feminine-looking sites or end up trawling the gay community's sites? That's how I define the community for my LifeOver35.com blog.

Then there are communities around particular interests. The job-seeking community is one which has unfortunately had very good reasons to be quite lively in recent years; in the bricks and mortar world you have job centres and head-hunting operations as well as a few employment bureaux and a massive industry in advertising vacancies.

Online, by adding social 'tags' to a set of jobs, you could make sure you're targeting the job-seeking professional PA community, or the job-seeking journalist community, or the job-seeking chef community. The fact that you suddenly have larger numbers to sift through means that a community which might be hard to reach through other channels becomes economically viable because you have eliminated geographical groupings as a factor. Approached correctly they should still respond as customers, opening up audiences to which you would otherwise have been closed.

So you can perceive communities where the members may themselves be unaware of it. And there are ways of engineering a bit of community feeling around the place.

Selecting the right network

You need to start by selecting the networks in which your customers and prospects are already taking part. Many businesses have suffered by going onto Twitter when their clients aren't there already, or onto Facebook in markets that have actively rejected that particular network.

You will need to find out which of the networks is right for your business by researching among your customers, as I established in my first book on the subject. Lots of companies audit their customers according to which media they read so that they can ascertain where to advertise; if you do this, ask them also where they get their social media and concentrate your fire wherever they congregate.

Various social media have different techniques to attract different communities and indeed to insulate uninterested people from stuff about which they're unmoved. Twitter's hashtags are a good, straightforward starting point.

Hashtags

You can actually force communities to happen – or set up the right conditions for them to occur naturally – on Twitter, still one of the fastest growing social networks you'll find. If you happen to have read my first book on social media you'll be aware that this started off as a series of announcements then really took off when it started to allow replies. It turned into a conversation.

The next step was when it turned into a series of conversations with the introduction of the hashtag, where you just put a hash sign – a '#' – in front of the subject you want to talk about. To many people this seems a bit pointless when the idea is first introduced, but it's not. The hashtag is a way of sorting through Tweets when you're using a fairly generic term. Let's say you're looking for, or offering, employment. So you enter '#jobs' as a search term into Twitter.

This search will yield a better result because it'll only show Tweets from people who've used the same #jobs hashtag. You'll still miss stuff, since not everyone will use that hashtag. For instance, you'll miss a Tweet that says 'Astrophysicist wanted, Tooting' because it doesn't have the word 'jobs' in it. But you'll get a better result because you've used a hashtag that people are likely to use.

TV and media programmes are wise to hashtags. They're displayed at the beginning so that people wanting to comment on, say, *The Apprentice*, UK or US version, will put the hashtag #apprentice into their Tweets so that someone can just follow those discussions whereas people wanting to discuss apprenticeships or find out about apprentices in general can exclude those Tweets from their system.

This helps enormously when looking for interest groups or communities. You're a toy manufacturer with a new license to offer figures based on the latest rash of superhero movies? Great, say so on Twitter and use the #Thor, #Batman, #Greenlantern, or whichever hashtag applies.

There's no central repository or decision-making body about what becomes a hashtag and what doesn't. It's all a bit random, they either take off or they don't – your followers adopt them or not. But they're a great start to finding when people have started to divide themselves into communities, which you can then target with relevant and non-intrusive advertising.

Hashtags that work, hashtags that don't

It's worth examining some of the real examples of hashtags people have used on Twitter which have worked and some of the others which have been less successful. It's worth excluding those intended as humorous; for example as I type I have Twitter open and someone has just posted a message with the hashtag #lazysunday – this isn't an entreaty to discuss lazy Sundays, it's someone demonstrating that they are relaxing. While I'm working. #bloodyannoying

The point there is that anybody can set up a hashtag for their own purposes. Some tend to catch light more than others. Blogger and event organizer Heidi Thorne reported on the straightnorth.com blog about finding colleagues to interact with. She found a search for a generic word like 'event' or 'events' offered too many results, not all of which were relevant to her job. Even adding a hashtag so she saw only examples in which people were drawing attention to an event, so searching for #event or #events, wasn't specific enough because it yielded too many people including suppliers, people attending events, and generally too much traffic.

By refining further and checking the now-defunct WhatTheHashtag. com for numbers of people following a particular hashtag, she found there were 475 people following the #eventprofs hashtag – which was a manageable number for her to interact with.

That particular site was no longer in use as this book went to press, but www.hashtag.com is a good place to start searching for hashtags including your particular keyword of preference.

Other networks

The other major networks don't have the same ease of creation as something like a hashtag but you can use a similar principle to search Facebook for groups of people discussing things in your business area. Make sure you tick the box for 'groups' when you're searching and then take part in any related discussions as your time allows.

LinkedIn also has groups and increasingly these are searchable and open. If someone still operates a closed group you'll need to ask them first before joining. You can set up your own group as well, if you have enough people ready to join. Never underestimate the work that goes into keeping these groups populated and fresh.

Getting the 'world wide' out of the web

Naturally not everybody wants to reach a world wide audience, but the world wide web – in spite of the name – is still useful to people wanting to reach only a narrow geographical community. People use Twitter, Facebook, LinkedIn, and the rest as well as the many local networks around to find people and businesses in their vicinity. This needn't be through particularly sophisticated means: often you'll see a note from someone on Twitter saying 'Can anyone recommend a good builder in Wigan,' or better still, 'Just had service from an excellent gardener in Brighton at a reasonable rate.' Of course someone can pretend to be a client and big their own service up, but you can find a lot out about local businesses by using the social networks.

Businesses can harness these social network members as well, and get them to operate as a sort of big marketing force – offering referrals and recommendations and using your hashtag to allow others to pick up on the services and goods you're offering.

One company that's done nicely through making a local community and interest group out of like-minded people is The Valet in Addiscombe, near Croydon in the UK. In early 2011 it won the Best New Business award for the Croydon heat of the South London Business Awards and it was shortlisted for the overall award.

Initially you'd think this was an ordinary if a little upmarket barber's shop. The signs are there – men sitting having their hair cut is a good clue but there are a few extras. There's a spa room on the premises where the business offers Swedish massages along with Indian stone treatments, facials, and other stuff. By the till the customers can buy the sorts of cologne, shaving creams, and upmarket shaving tools for which they'd normally have to travel to Central London or – let's be honest – to their Amazon account, where you can get most of it.

This seemed to be a business in which the clients would welcome the chance to feel part of some sort of membership (otherwise why not just get the retail stuff online), and owner/founder David Maseyk takes a multi-channel approach – this book's focus is electronic marketing but in the real world it's all about getting the right mix.

'At present we run a loyalty scheme,' he says. 'It's a membership thing, makes the client feel like they're part of a club – we offer loyalty points [which exchange for discounts or service upgrades] against treatments and product purchases. Once the customer has reached a total of 100 points they're entitled to redeem them for exchange.' Customers bring their membership cards out every time they pay for something, which is an interesting psychological point as there's really no need – the salon will have taken the name when it booked the appointment so adding the points is going to happen automatically. It's part of that feeling of belonging to something.

Electronic marketing is also very important to the company. It has a YouTube channel where it demonstrates a relaxing barbershop shave among other things, a lively Facebook page where it announces offers, an e-newsletter which goes to as many customers as require it, and a Twitter account to keep in touch with customers as well. 'It's like I've got two projects, one is called The Valet Barber and the other is the Facebook, Twitter, and our business blog marketing side of it,' says Maseyk.

He spends time with his outsourced marketing company on other elements of e-marketing:

- **Google Adwords** – This is a scheme in which Google offers sponsored click-throughs – a business pays a small amount every time a potential customer clicks through after searching for a particular term. Maseyk found paying per click didn't result in a paying customer every time.

- **Spending time on SEO** – this has performed better. Wisely he asks customers how they found the company when they weren't physically walking past, and a lot of them reply 'Internet search.' The Valet is careful to note what the customer was searching for and tweaks the website to attract more (when the interview took place the business had done well from people looking for 'men's facial Croydon' for example, coming out ahead of many longer established competitors.)

- **Using incoming links** – this pushes a site up the search ranking so the company ensures that the Facebook page leads back to the website, the blog leads back to Facebook, and the Tweets lead to both so there's a little continuum of electronic marketing. The website is 'thevaletmalegrooming.com' and having 'male grooming' as a keyword in the title has also helped SEO.

Maseyk is realistic about the commitment that running his customers as an electronic community of some sort actually involves, and confirms it's not easy. He is well aware that a lively Facebook community will pay as customers return to it for advice and exchange ideas about, say, shaving products, and if he's there to stoke the conversations it'll do even better. 'The problem is I'm overstretched already,' he explains. 'We've grown the business for two years, it's pulling into profit and so you're pulled in different directions. I could downgrade something else to make cuts in order to divert my attention to the social media side of things, but that wouldn't do any justice as you market to draw new business, but you then need to provide the service you're advertising to retain that business. I don't want to compromise the current business model we have on the floor, so it's a case of having to delegate the work properly amongst a committed team, but in a nut shell the social media side of things is a key element to keeping the business and our customers in tune.'

Funding and managing

This is the conundrum facing most small business owners. Often it's simply difficult to find the time to engage with the customer and prospective customer online. You might aim to thank people on Twitter every time they give your business a mention, but if you're busy trying to build up new business, it just doesn't always happen. Likewise with keeping the Facebook community running for your business.

This is a universal problem. I was speaking at an educational publisher's event on social media in 2010 and one of the people attending explained that he didn't have extra resources to conjure up. He couldn't allocate people he didn't have or hire someone extra when his budget was actually being cut, so was struggling to make social media work for him with the overstretched skeleton staff he actually had.

The answer is a very old-fashioned one – time management and focusing on what is achievable and what isn't. You might want to draw yourself up a list of tasks: these would include your core business functions, admin, sales, marketing, liaising with professional advisors, all the things a business has to do. Then add the desirable things: exorting people to review your business on websites and how they might be persuaded to do this without falling foul of the Bribery Act or ASA. Then allocate time to each task, see how 'overdrawn' you actually are on the time available to you and start cutting out the inessential tasks. At the same time it would be useful to put a table together of how much your business gets out of individual tasks to see whether there are any unproductive areas you can cut to make time for the newer stuff.

Masyek admits to suffering from this overstretchedness but despite this, The Valet scores better than most High Street retail premises for social networking and online community building. Ask anyone who has to handle the back office of such a business and be there for customers and they'll confirm that being social electronically as well is damned tough.

The Bribery Act

That got your attention – bribery! In 2011 the UK became subject to the Bribery Act, and this could lead to some grey areas when it comes to asking your customers to review something for you, or Tweet positively, or any of those other things designed to get new people walking in through the door.

Essentially if you're offering any incentive or inducement for a positive review, the review itself should say so in some way. This is going to be tricky in a 140-character Tweet, although many PR people are getting around it by using the hashtag #client (which works as shorthand for 'I am writing this positive stuff about a client'). Perhaps something comparable will evolve for incentivized Tweets.

It's all about openness and not representing things as independent views when they're no such thing. Remember this if you're offering customers discounts or a freebie if they leave a good review somewhere. They will almost certainly be covered by the Act.

You might also want to consider, once people are aware you're effectively paying for good coverage, just how seriously the other customers and prospects are going to take it. Bribery Act or not, If I know someone's being rewarded in some way contingent on a good review I'm not likely to believe the review.

Peer reviews

There are a number of areas on the Internet in which customers can post reviews of a service. If you encourage customers to go onto these and put a review in place, great – be aware, though, that the reviews will by definition be beyond your control. If someone thinks they've had a lousy haircut at The Valet they'll say so, regardless of looking fine in everyone else's eyes.

The more reviews you get, as a rule, the more credible they seem. The trick is not to worry too much about whether an individual review is good or bad and watch the trend and the numbers. If loads of people are reviewing you well, great – if one or two had a bad experience people are likely to believe the rest of the reviews.

The Valet scores dramatically in the local networking arena, and this is where a lot of smaller outlets can do extremely well. Maseyk has seen to it that customers can find (figures correct at the time of writing and they can only grow):

- Google Maps (54 reviews)

- Review Centre (44 reviews)

- Trusted Places by Yell (9 reviews)

- Whose View (6 reviews)

- TouchLocal.com (11 reviews)

- Facebook (28 reviews).

This peer review system gets a lot of customers motivated to visit premises designed for them and reviewed by like-minded people, presumably looking for the same sort of service as the reader. The reviews are highlighted on the website and this again makes for a critical mass – a sort of virtuous circle of positive reviews placed where customers are deciding where to buy.

Registering for the local sites

The question for many small businesses reading will be: how do Maseyk and businesses like his get onto these local networks in the first place? The easiest way to start is to do a search on your immediate competition and see where they're being reviewed.

There's a lot of chicken and egg going on here. Take the Whoseview.co.uk site for example. The Valet has six reviews on it partly because it has encouraged people to leave them there but also because they just felt like doing so. You can 'claim' a business on the site if someone has reviewed yours or you can add your business (both have costs attached). Anyone reading this who has a small business serving a local community – or a large business with branches doing the same – should have a look immediately and see if it's already there so you can consider replying to negative reviews or better, thanking people for positive ones (although do have a look at the box on negative comments).

Review Centre operates differently; its finances are driven by advertising and there's no charge for having your business set up on the site. Just ask them through their website and they'll do it in 14 days, or ask a customer to write a review (they may be doing so already). Yell.com, likewise, with its Trusted Places, encourages people to upload reviews immediately they arrive on the site with no invitation to register to have your business examined.

Proactively encouraging your community

This could all sound a bit scary because it's completely beyond your control. You can ask people to leave a review but will they? Likewise will it be a review you wish they hadn't written?

There are plenty of things you can do which can be kept within control. Most of the energy around your business is going to come from you, to be honest, rather than your customers, so the more noise you make about it the better. As Masyek said previously, the sense of participation is important. Customers at The Valet are encouraged to convert to some sort of active membership. There is the aforementioned redundant membership card. Members' accounts are kept up to date and loyalty points awarded at the till – you don't have to produce a card but customers like to do so.

There is also an e-newsletter which highlights not only individual staff members but also occasionally customers. If someone is doing something for charity it may get a mention or, as was the case at A Suit That Fits, the odd celebrity popping in will get a mention. More importantly, however, people are encouraged to write a review of the service on the sites mentioned above

E-newsletter contents

Source: www.thevaletmalegrooming.com used with permission of The Valet.

If you're going to send out a newsletter then good – do it. But plan it first, and don't just think about the first couple of issues. Consider the frequency – maybe ask some customers how often they'd like to hear from you (they're unlikely to have much of an idea but you can mention the fact that you've asked when you come to the launch) – then try planning out your first three months' content. It has to be easy to read, it has to be correctly spelled or people will think you're amateurish, and above all there has to be something going on so you can fill it.

Then there's the business planning. How long is this going to take in addition to your Facebooking, Tweeting, and other social networking, your cajoling of customers to write reviews and engaging in conversation with them electronically? Once you have that amount of time in your head or on paper there's the small matter of how much your income has to go up before it's worth doing and how long you're prepared to wait while the revenue reaches that point.

You may not be after revenue as such. Let's take the existing example of The Valet. David Maseyk sends out his newsletters periodically; he and his web master have got the hang of RSS feeds so people get sent the thing either to their news reader or by email. Would someone really want their hair cut or a shave more often than before because of a newsletter, though? The answer is almost certainly not. They might, though, feel more loyalty to The Valet than somewhere that didn't keep them up to date and treat them as a part of something that was fun to take part in.

So set your target realistically.

Outsourcing the newsletter

If you have a web designer and want your newsletter to look consistent with your website then obviously get them to do it (and the more consistency the better). As with any marketing effort a good method is to start with your desired outcome and work backwards from there. You want sales, start by writing the sales close and work the design around that. You want them to come to your website, you make it very branded and maybe have some unfinished articles so if they want to finish reading they've got to go to the main site.

If you have more basic design requirements take a look at mailchimp. com. This is a free service which has a number of templates on offer so that you can make your newsletter look great. It also has the facility to manage your mailing lists.

And I do mean 'manage.' Its reports will tell you who opened your newsletter and which parts of it they clicked. This is automatic, instant feedback on which parts of your content are gaining traction and which aren't. It also tells you what they did after they finished reading – just close the newsletter, click through to another link on your site? Go to one of your affiliates?

This is valuable marketing data about the people you're trying to attract and it's easy to get at because someone else has done the coding for you. All you need to do is to log onto your account.

Making it seem individual

Finally your business needs to look at its electronic and social media promotions, memberships or however you wish to look at them, as an adjunct to an existing business. Too many companies get carried away with every last small piece of marketing that comes their way; they can end up as career marketers rather than wine sellers, gardeners, photographers, or whatever they planned to become in the first place.

This is where David Maseyk, stretched though he may be, is getting it very right indeed. He can't allocate the time both to running an excellent social media campaign or Facebook interactions as well as running the business without cutting corners; at the time of writing he hadn't the resources to outsource the social media elements to anybody else so he took the decision that the service and its personalization came first. He doesn't do as much Tweeting and Facebooking as he'd like because it would take him away from looking after his customers and suppliers and without an excellent service he might as well go home.

Electronic marketing can help in this personalization. Finding out what people are looking at and what they are ignoring on a newsletter tells you where your focus needs to be. Seeing where they go on your website after reading your newsletter can be instructive in telling you whether you've missed something, whether they're more inclined to spend money. Good branding will help, and so will little touches like putting someone's name on a newsletter rather than an impersonal 'dear customer.' But it should certainly tell you how to make the electronic experience of your business closer to the feeling of actually being there.

Community

This chapter started by talking about the sort of community your customers belong to. We went through a few possibilities of ethnicity, age, and sex, then we looked at the way they divide themselves into communities along the lines of interests without even thinking about it.

However if there's one technique or idea I'd like you to take away from this chapter then it's that they're also in another community – the community of your customers. They join immediately they step through the door and they become a member of the community of your prospects when they start to look at your website. Turning these community members into active rather than passive ones, by engaging with them wherever possible and keeping in touch through e-newsletters and tracking what they do about these communications is a vital part of social commerce in the loosest sense.

Action points

- Follow a few customers on Twitter if they're there. See if they have any interests which help you catch their attention for further business.

- Use hashtags as described in this chapter. Look at setting up a hashtag for your own company.

- Consider engaging with customers through a newsletter and as in The Valet's example, leading people between the different networks so they become immersed in your e-community.

- Look at Mailchimp and the marketing data you can get from this newsletter.

- Manage your time – you need a target for these marketing engagements and you need to be sure your time spent on them is worthwhile.

7 NEW PRODUCT DEVELOPMENT AND CUSTOMER SERVICE

Developing a product or service the customer wants is something I see very much linked to caring for the customer after purchase. So in this chapter we're going to look at using your social media connections to develop new products and to work on customer service. You can 'crowdsource' what they want, in other words literally source the information you need from the crowd of people following you.

Customers also ask sensible questions, thank goodness. They ask things that improve stuff. And thanks to social networking they can do it en masse so you know it's not just a rogue eccentric who wants, say, lavender-flavoured toothpaste (one of the companies quoted in this book actually sells that, and I'll send a £10 Amazon voucher to whoever emails me and tells me which one it is first – seriously, ten quid, that's probably almost £1 more than you paid for this book in the first place).

So in this chapter you'll walk through:

- How to engage with customers in the first place so that you find out what they really want

- How you can start to develop products through asking many prospects, really inexpensively

- Finding good ideas compared to the ideas which will waste your time

- Sustaining a corporate voice throughout your communications and finding what the customers will respond to

- Understanding that every piece of communication is now part of your customer service

- Getting it right at the recruitment stage.

Sanity check: who are you listening to?

This is of course a social media book. There are good reasons for this. Millions of people use social media and if you play the game, talk to them like individuals rather than droids who might hand their money over if you're lucky, have some fun and entertainment with them, you can save a lot of money on market research.

That only leaves the people who don't use social media to appease. And the people who use it but only to stay in touch with their family and friends. There is a much larger world out there and you need to bear in mind that for the moment, social media users are likely to be:

- Affluent – particularly if they're using the technology on the move they're owners of smartphones.
- Technology-savvy – for the moment at least it's only the technologized who're using this stuff in depth.

If that sounds like your customers, great. If it doesn't then you need to use social media research as part of, not all of, your research and development effort.

Brave new products – a word about research and development

Huge amounts of money go into research and development of new product offerings and the refinements of existing ones. Very few products emerge from businesses on the strength of 'seat of the pants' logic; the market is researched first to find out if there's a gap, then if there's a willing audience. Packaging, price, size – everything that requires investment into the final look and feel of an offering will ultimately be up to the market research. There are a number of ways of handling this in the traditional business world and they are still valid. The market researcher either standing in the street with a clipboard or hitting the phones and talking to the prospective customer. The focus group, in which a number of people are gathered together and discuss what they'd really like from the product. Both options can be very scientific when done properly. They should not be discounted just because the social option is now available.

Social media can, however, save a lot of expenditure on this area.

'Ice cream, you scream'

One example of a company that changed its offerings as a direct result of social media was QVC UK. The company is well known for its shopping channels on television internationally but on this occasion it was selling through its website and added customer ratings and reviews, to engage customers but also to get some informal feedback on the products people were buying.

Agency BazaarVoice set up the interaction and quickly gained more than 300,000 reviews of products over the network. The people were definitely interested in taking part.

An unexpected bonus was the emergence of the social media as a sort of early warning system. There was feedback on household appliances which enabled the manufacturer to take action and rectify it, and a handful of feedback on a particular perfume was enough to persuade the vendor – rightly – that it was a dud batch.

More helpfully, one popular ice cream maker had no returns at all and no customer complaints, so QVC thought it was doing well. It continued to feature it both online and on television. Immediately the reviews started, however, the company realized it had a problem. Not only was it not doing the job but it was damaging the brand; customers reported in reviews that they were surprised QVC stocked anything so poor, but for the money they'd paid they didn't want to kick up a fuss, they were simply binning them – while the presenters were extolling their virtues as the latest must-have bargain.

Through social media feedback QVC found it needed to discontinue the sale of the item and focus on genuinely well-performing goods that would enhance its own brand value.

The customer is always right?

Loads of people spend a great deal of money on product development and customer service, both online and off. There are a few examples in which products have been developed without any real need just because the customers said they thought it would be a good idea. Famously in the early 1990s Amstrad, then primarily owned by Alan (now Lord) Sugar, was reported in the press as having computers overheating. The company disputed that this was happening and said it had received no complaints but the customer furore was such that it ended up putting fans in anyway. Lord Sugar made a comment in a statement to the effect that 'We don't need fans, but if the customer wants fans we'll have them put in.' This quote came back to haunt him when he bought Tottenham Hotspur, but I digress.

Other feedback has been useful to a large number of businesses. Again in the 1990s I once interviewed a company that made network routers – obviously not the tiny broadband beasts we have now but a slightly larger affair with lots of wires and lights. I asked: if the network is working and you can get a console on your screen to see all the data coming in and going out, why do you need all those lights? Because, they said, when we released one without the lights the customers came back to us and asked 'why can't we see the lights coming on any more to show us the network's come on?'

So they put the lights back. And Lord Sugar put the fans back in. There are probably many other examples too in the annals of business history, in which the crowd has felt it needs something when actually it doesn't – it can pay to listen to them regardless.

The tone before social

Innocent Drinks, a UK-based smoothies company, has been a social company for some time now. It has a particular personality which reflects in everything from the Twitter feed to the website and even the product packaging. It's worth taking a little while to elaborate on the sort of corporate atmosphere that exists in the business. A few years ago I was editing an annual book on *Britain's Top Employers*. I visited Innocent during my research. The first time I went, there was a notice above the door that said 'Visitors' – and one above the window that said 'Burglars.' The meeting room in which my interview took place was made – flooring, furniture, everything – out of recycled tyres.

On my second visit, just over a year later, the signs and tyres had vanished, but they had astroturfed the reception area following a vote on what sort of floor covering to go and get. Then to celebrate this they astroturfed the outside of a couple of their delivery vans.

I haven't visited since. Frankly I'd be nervous of what I might find next. Reactions are of course divided; either you'll love the idea and think 'when can I start?' or you'll really, really hate the corporate culture and the idea of working in such a place just won't appeal.

Entering a conversation

This gives you the backdrop to a company that started life before any of this social media stuff began as a bit of an oddball. As a business, it believes it has been 'social' for longer than the technology that we know as 'social media' or 'social networking' has actually existed. Quite unusually the organization invites people to phone up, any time, just for a chat sometimes. Joe McEwan is currently head of engagement for the company and he believes this is what made the business a natural candidate for the more modern social engagement. 'We want to show people that if they want to chat, then we're here to listen about anything,' he says. 'You don't have to have a product fault to get in touch with us because we're open and friendly enough to just chat.'

Odd though it might sound to someone who wasn't expecting customers to have a conversation with someone who was paid to sit and chat, the idea was a success. Innocent was doing this before anyone was talking about having 'conversations' with their customers and a lot of people will have seen the idea as outright lunacy. But in making this work, there's an argument that says Innocent anticipated what would later become the entire social media concept from the commercial point of view. It shared so much in common with it:

- Commercially irrelevant conversations as part of the business

- Impossibility of tracking the exact commercial impact

- Deliberate informality throughout the company including the packaging.

It remains pretty much impossible to say why this sort of activity should have a positive impact on a business but by now it's pretty certain that it does. Others have copied, and McEwan welcomes this. 'I'd like to think we talk better nonsense than most,' he adds. The company refers to the content as 'conversation currency' – just chat about stuff people find interesting.

Having all but fallen into social media before social media were really established, Innocent found quite quickly that it was a natural move to make the communications electronic when the market started to move that way. It was one of the earlier practitioners but as with a number of its business practices it broke a few of the rules. Specifically, as McEwan confirms, there isn't a deliberate business plan or strategy behind the idea, it's just an extension of something the company has always done. That said, it does offer benefits from the customer care point of view and indeed from product development.

Payback time: the research

So if there's no actual strategy how does any of this stuff work? On the customer service front it's important to put this into the context of the rest of the operation. Emails, phone calls, and letters are logged and tracked through a system the company has been using for a while and social media now feeds into that. 'We have a great little system that we call Bertha that enables us to track and specify to quite a fine level of detail the nature of someone's call. So we know exactly what it is that they were happy about, or what it is they were asking us about, or what it is they didn't like about a product or something that we were doing,' says McEwan. 'And we've always monitored that feedback quite closely, and tried to learn from it, so something that Twitter and Facebook and other channels help us to do is to understand what people think about the things we're doing across a much broader spectrum.'

The impact on all businesses is potentially huge. McEwan's belief is that the idea of surveying a mass market, of looking into focus groups for the granular stuff and checking out the larger market research to find out what the trends are, have been severely modified if they're not changed all together. What's really altered is that a business can now talk directly to its customers in very large numbers.

Not that the older forms of research are dead. 'You get different forms of contact through the different channels,' says McEwan. It's not right to look just at the mass market stuff, he says, nor to think 'people are emailing on this subject so that's the big one' nor indeed to think 'our Facebook page says this is very important so presumably that's what we should be addressing.' 'If you glue all those together, then you get a much clearer and fairer and broader picture of what people are saying,' he continues. 'So we put what people are saying to us on the phone or on Twitter or on Facebook on the same kind of pedestal as we do the results of much larger survey based market research.'

This sort of mix ends up informing the business of what it needs to do for as many customers as possible, as long as they're engaging with the company. As a business strategy it is inevitably riven with gaps because nobody can be certain a particular set of customers will want to engage, so of course you end up listening to the more voluble ones who are on the various media. This is why the more traditional forms of research, which target people who haven't necessarily come forward as self-appointed spokespeople, remain important.

Of course none of this is free. In my previous book I spoke about planning for the actual cost of social media rather than falling for the 'it's free to join Twitter so it doesn't cost anything' flannel a lot of people push out there; it's free only if you value your time and that of your colleagues at zero. This is an issue of which McEwan and his colleagues are well aware.

Costs

He compares an advertisement to a firework. It shoots up in the air, makes a lot of noise and light and then it's over until someone shoots another firework up in the air. Social media, he suggests, is more akin to a bonfire. 'Fireworks are impressive but they're over very quickly. Social media is like a bonfire. Lots of people come together to build a fire and it lasts for a much longer time,' he says. 'And actually, in terms of going to see fireworks and going to a bonfire, if you go to a bonfire you tend to stay for longer. It's a warmer, more personal experience where you get talking to more people, if you know what I mean.'

Before the metaphor collapses under its own weight it's worth paraphrasing him a little more. A good mix of marketing absolutely needs those big pyrotechnics and displays or people will get bored with it, but you need to cater for the customers who want the more intimate, warmer experience. You need to be prepared to pay people for their time focusing on all of these components.

Product research

And of course it can start to pay handsomely. Innocent doesn't only make smoothies, it has diversified – slightly – into veg pots. It has seasonal as well as permanent ranges and like all commercial companies it listens to its customers' feedback. Social engagement means that it can get this feedback more immediately than any unengaged competition. 'To be completely blunt, we had one particular mushroom based veg pot recipe that just wasn't performing that well,' says McEwan. This contrasted with a piri piri based guest recipe that was doing better than anticipated. 'Consumers were giving it great feedback on the rate and review section of our website, it was getting great feedback on Twitter, it was getting lots of positive comments on Facebook. By keeping an eye on these channels on a daily basis we could see that people loved the piri piri product,' says McEwan. 'We then pulled that data together, and did some comparative analysis to show that the piri piri recipe was being much better received than the mushroom recipe and this gave us our business case. So we replaced the mushroom recipe with piri piri. Simple stuff really, but stuff that other businesses often neglect.'

This is called crowd sourcing: put a message out into the crowd and ask for feedback and you'll get more than one answer which you can start to build into some sort of overview. Crowd sourcing can apply to more than information – earlier in the book I discussed crowd funding, which is a variation on the same principle in which a group of people fund a business. You could apply it elsewhere as well,

And of course the company was in a position to act on its findings. 'We saw something was happening, e.g. people loved the piri piri product,' says McEwan. 'We then pulled that data together, put some numbers behind it, put it in relation to how the previous recipe fared against it during the three month period we were examining. After that we had our business case, so we turned it into a permanent recipe and got rid of mushroom because that was just doing less well.'

This doesn't happen overnight. If you are part of a business, you need a solid method to pull all of the data together. You need to apportion weighting to the various inputs you're going to get, and you need the ear of management and decision makers to make the changes suggested. You might put together a diagram like this:

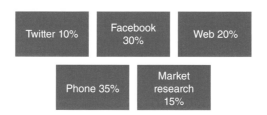

Those numbers could be way off beam but they illustrate how you might start apportioning the importance of different sorts of input into a company's products. It's a suggested start of a framework to support decisions in a business. Let's say you sell musical instruments and sheet music in a shop and the online side has been growing. You might consider:

● Personal customers offer immediate feedback but account for only 30% of the business compared to 60% last year – so they need a lower weighting.

● Telephone feedback normally comes from people calling with an issue – this is important but it will skew any feedback so they also need a lower rating.

● Facebook is voluble but accounts for only 20% of your sales so that also gets a low rating – but higher than telephone.

● Twitter customers have almost always bought from you and are a growing number so you give them more weight.

. . . and so forth. You'll need to work out your own metrics to fit your own business but it's a way of allocating the appropriate weight to each channel from which you get feedback.

That said, if you find the personal customers are all complaining while people on Twitter are delighted with the service you might want to see whether there's an underlying problem!

Content and tone

What's really distinctive about Innocent is, as I've hinted earlier in this chapter, the personality the company puts on display just about the whole time. There are, to be honest, a lot of people who are a little too informal and over-familiar on the social networks. The 'what I've had for breakfast' brigade have become such a cliché it's not worth repeating; equally pernicious are the people who'll tell you they've just got out of the shower (depending on who you are I may not welcome the mental image), are just about to put the dinner on, and so forth. There is a surprisingly large amount of that still around, even on some business feeds.

Innocent notes that it's the people who offer the most amusing or interesting content who end up getting followed the most and are considered the most influential. This could mean they're linking to some interesting stuff on the Web, or just saying things that make people laugh. 'We got massive engagement with a Facebook post and Tweet about fish films the other day. We were having a chat here in the office, coming up with different films and changing the title of the film subtly to make a fish film. Like "The Codfather," or "Bulletproof Monkfish." We asked people to come up with their own and had hundreds of likes and comments from consumers. Some absolute gems like Loach Cassidy and the Sundance Squid.' People joined in from all over the plaice (see what I did there?). 'I think it's good to post things that have nothing to do with what you do or for you to be promoting something else altogether because it's a privilege that people have decided to let you into their Facebook news feed. You have to be really careful because if what you're putting into that news feed is boring, or annoying, it only takes one click to unlike a brand,'

Recruitment is king

Getting people who are on the right wavelength is vital, of course. This is why I went into so much detail about the backdrop earlier in this chapter; one of the positive things about Innocent's recruitment process is that if a candidate walks in and they aren't in tune with the organization there's a very good chance they'll walk straight out again. 'We've always recruited against our five company values. They're all equally important but if I had to pick one that really stands out for me it's natural. We use natural ingredients to make all natural products that are good for you, but natural is also about being yourself. It's about being natural in the way we communicate with each other, so it's about honesty and being genuine,' explains McEwan. 'Particularly in the roles where writing in the Innocent tone is part of a job. For those roles we take extra care to recruit people who are comfortable communicating naturally, and comfortable being themselves. You shouldn't always have to change who you are to suit a business. People work better when they're encouraged to be themselves.' In fact part of the training, which still comes from the same man who wrote the labels in the first place, is not to try too hard. If staff make an effort to capture the Innocent tone and then redraft to get it right, the chances are it's not going to work.

Recruitment, then, needs to take into account the tone and someone's ability and willingness to engage. Underpinning this is a philosophy that customer service has expanded. Every engagement, every interaction with the customer is some sort of service you are offering even if it's not labelled 'customer service.' An attempt to make them smile, a piece of product branding which would previously have come under the 'marketing' banner, you're engaging with individuals now so there's a lot more service happening with each online transaction.

Does it work?

The chances are that all of this helps drive Innocent's sales and would do the same for any business similarly getting it right. There is a proviso, and that is that you needn't expect success in social media to be measurable exactly if you go through indirect channels like retailers.

That is, you can measure your 'success' in pure social media terms, You can establish how many people retweet your stuff, you can look into how many Facebook comments and 'likes' you get but none of this matters a very great deal when it comes to the bottom line business figures. For all the analytics available I believe there is one figure that's going to matter to a business when it's evaluating its social media engagement, and that figure is the profit. If it's up after a social media engagement, and preferably a higher margin than before, then it's a successful engagement. If it's not, or worse, if it's down, then the engagement has been at best a lukewarm success even if everyone's Facebooking and Tweeting you like crazy people.

And an indirect channel adds another complication. Earlier in the book we discussed Penderyn, the distillers in Wales, and how impossible it was to say whether a customer had picked up a bottle in a supermarket because they were familiar with the brand through Facebook or for any other reason. The same will be true of Innocent and anyone else who can't track precisely what the customer is doing and thinking at the point of purchase.

So your analytics really need one thing in them. Is the business doing any better since we started this stuff? And if not, why not?

Listening to what works

There are – I hope – a number of learnings to take away from this chapter. First, customer research has to be king even when you know the customers are wrong. Alan Sugar rescuing sales by putting a spurious fan into his computers is an amusing story but also a mark of a wise businessperson who understood that addressing the surface concern would be easier and less expensive than marketing the fact that the computers weren't overheating in the first place.

It's also more important than ever to understand that your customer perception needs to be underpinned by an excellent service or product or else you might as well shut the business and go home. Innocent has done extremely well through a number of means. First it fell into the social business because it was already a social company. Nobody else, literally nobody (unless a reader knows better) had set up a for-profit business and put in a phone line for people who just fancied a natter. If social media hadn't become so big we'd still be writing them off as a bunch of hippie weirdos (oh come on, we were all thinking it). But it anticipated something much bigger and was well equipped to deal with it when it arrived.

And it was willing to look at what worked in the new media rather than to be too prescriptive. Getting in early allowed it time to let the new stuff breathe for a while. Crucially the company understood that this was a new part of the mix and a great way of talking to customers but that it wasn't a substitute for the market researcher approaching non-customers in the street and getting their views as well, or asking people something specific in the concentrated atmosphere of a focus group.

It found that listening enabled it to respond when particular products were going well and to withdraw them when they weren't. It saved money on this sort of research and by detecting the trend early on it cut the amount of redundant inventory it could have had and pushed resources into more profitable areas. It also found that people responded well to a consistent voice rather than having the dad-dancing-at-a-wedding style engagements some corporate businesses have adopted when facing the social media for the first time. And it understood that in order for any of this to work, the business had to be working in the first place and this goes back as far as the recruitment process.

Action points

You might not be an Innocent (or you might) but there will be ways of getting your customers to feed back into the product development and service process:

- Have a look at the way you monitor the market at the moment and stick to it. Social media and social commerce activities should augment this, not replace it.

- Listen to any underlying messages and look for trends that your questions might not have uncovered. Remember Innocent didn't ask 'are there any of our products you don't warm to,' it asked for general chat and picked up on trends.

- Engage on social media in a way that suits your business. Try not to make it look forced.

- Listen to the responses and act. Use it as market testing – if enough people hate a product or service, scrap it. If they love it, make more. Simple.

- Build an awareness of the sort of engagement you want to encourage into your recruitment process. It needs to go that far back if you're going to get the tone right.

8 MARKETING COMMUNICATIONS

It seems so obvious that social media is a good way of performing marketing communications that it's almost not worth saying. And yet so many people keep getting it wrong – or if that sounds too strident then perhaps we could agree there are people who manage their communications in a way that really can't be deemed helpful.

Take the candidate at a social media seminar I hosted after the launch of my first book, who was herself an author. She had been excited to note that her publisher had gone onto Twitter for the first time, and imagined her name in lights, the publisher doing everything it could to make the most of the sales of her latest novel. She logged on to find the only entry said: 'Muriel's just eaten three Twix.'

And yet I wonder whether that's really all that bad. Suppose, for example, the publisher had a reputation for being stuffy. Maybe it was one of those officious organizations that appears to lack a human face – in which case Muriel and her Twix (names and confectionery bars changed to protect the guilty) might have given the brand just the lift it needed. I mean, I doubt it, but it's possible.

Other organizations with which I've worked and consulted have bigger issues than someone in the office posting something not all that interesting. There's the issue of exactly who should handle the social media activities in an organization, for example. If there are ten of you then that's fine, you can decide between you. If there are 10,000 spread across different countries and, crucially, different cultures, it's a different question. There are issues about cross-culture communication; something that sounds a little self-deprecating and humorous to the British audience could sound wrong if it's interpreted literally. In her excellent book *Watching the English: the Hidden Rules of Business Behaviour* Kate Fox points to the example of someone from Germany asking an English person what he or she does for a living. The English person starts 'Oh, this and that' and the German assumes it is literally true that the English person doesn't do a lot; meanwhile the English person was expecting to be asked a bit more and then to confirm that they were doing staggeringly well.

This sort of issue crops up a lot on social media as well as in the 'real world.' And it is in this chapter that we will work through some of those issues as well as put forward some best practice. In this chapter you should:

- Learn to recognize your 'digital shadow' and understand the importance of this

- Start to build your brand using your digital profile

- Use your digital outputs for reputation management and damage control

- Consider the reputations you can't control, and how to react to them

- Learn how not to be seen as manipulative by these outside people

- Learn to interact with bloggers as a subset of the above.

Your digital shadow

Digital marketing agency supremo Anthony Mayfield has written an excellent book called *Me and my Web Shadow*. He seeks to answer one question throughout (this is my emphasis, not his): what happens when someone enters your name into the Google search engine?

For 'name' you can read 'company name' as well. So, how often do you Google yourself? For a lot of people the answer is 'not much.' They consider – for good reason – that they, not some other commentator, are the expert on themselves and their company, so nobody else can or should advise them on what's being said.

Hmm. True enough on the face of it. But what about a friend of a friend – true story and no it's not me – who had a female employee declare she was going to take him to court for sexual harassment. He was bewildered as he considered himself innocent; she said he had made indecent advances and went to the press.

He did some digging. He found out that she had done this to a number of employers before and rather than be dragged through the courts they had caved in and settled for a few thousand pounds. He'd confronted her, she'd backed down of course and resigned. No actual harm done but a nasty taste in the mouth.

Oh, and the web stuff. As I mentioned, she'd been to the local press, which of course had reported – carefully – the fact that there was going to be a hearing of some sort. So every time someone entered my friend-of-a-friend's name in Google, the allegation about sexual abuse came up. Of course the press ran a follow-up but due to the nature of search engine optimization it appeared on Google page 2.

So he ended up carrying a sheaf of cuttings around with him so anyone who'd Googled him would know beyond doubt that he'd been exonerated. I'm telling you this because there could be something out there about you that's not true either – and you might not know about it. The following are genuine examples:

- In 1989 an accounting company called Multisoft was bought. A UK newspaper mis-reported this as Microsoft (before that was a household name).

- At the time of writing Venezuelan President Hugo Chavez is alive and well. Unless you believed Twitter reports in June 2011, which said he had died.

- On 25 June 2009 the singer Michael Jackson died, very prematurely. On the same day the social media were alive with rumours that tragically, actor Jeff Goldblum had also passed away. Goldblum, like Chavez, had done no such thing and I wish him continued good health.

My point isn't that there's a right load of nonsense on the Internet if you look hard enough. You knew that. My point is that if something inaccurate is said about you, you need to do something about it because unlike the press in the Multisoft example above, someone will have archived it somewhere online and it's going to come up in a search.

This is what I mean by your digital shadow and what Mayfield calls your web shadow. We live online increasingly and we're leaving traces. Just try Googling yourself or your company and see what you find if you've been around for a while. You might find any of the following:

- Old Tweets and emails

- Your Facebook or LinkedIn page

- Old/archived press releases

- Old presentations you made and forgot you'd shared with people online at the time.

Any of these can damage or enhance your business. There won't be a lot you can do about them unless you're still with the company, but you can certainly start planning for posterity now. A few basic rules should help:

- Don't trash the competition

- Don't make rash predictions

- Be corporate rather than individual when you're writing about business

- If someone has put an awkward picture of you on Facebook, untag it.

The reasons are straightforward. Your prediction that the iPad will fall out of fashion and that we'll go back to using slates might be right but if it's wrong some journalist is going to ask you about it – or an awkward customer will reproduce it on your web page and there will be nothing you can do about it. Unless, of course, you're still in charge of the site on which it appears. Trashing the competition is bad practice anyway, particularly if they may one day hire you or buy your company.

You get the idea. This stuff sticks. You need to take control or to have an answer as to why the truth (or your opinion of it) has changed. This is particularly important if you use an agency for your social media engagements; you can sign off all sorts of controversial stuff without meaning to if you're not careful.

Before social media became widespread there was a managing director of a laptop computer company (in the days when these cost thousands). He was quoted in a press release as saying the desktop computer was dead. Inevitably he went to work for a desktop computer company, so I ran the quote past him. He said it was a good little jab, but he never said the desktop was dead.

I went back to the office and checked. He'd been quoted saying it in a press release, I had it in black and off-white. But I recognize he was probably right, he never actually said it. Best guess is that a PR company came up with what sounded like (and was) a lively quote so he signed it off. Before social media this was one thing; if he did something similar now the quote would be all around the globe, following him and being retweeted.

Be aware of your digital past. Be aware of misconceptions by all means, but be even more aware of the accurate stuff and have an answer for it!

Corporate digital: Sage advice

Software company Sage has been using social media for a couple of years. It has 800,000 customers in the UK, all of whom are businesses and they use the company for accounting, customer relationship management, health and safety advice, and a great deal more.

Digital PR manager Cath Sheldon's brief is to work across all of these divisions so she builds the brand throughout the organization.

. Her role (she was an internal candidate) came about because of the way customers had started wanting to engage with the company. 'The first stage was about sort of listening and learning,' she explains. 'It was about discovering what our competitors were doing, what our customers expected from us online outside of our own website and where we could really add value to that.' This is of course standard stuff, as was the next stage, establishing which social networks to join. Twitter and YouTube were deemed the most obvious.

What's noticeable about Sage, though, is the sheer size of the business. Its head office is in Newcastle where it employs about 1000 people; there are more through the country and indeed overseas. It became important very quickly to decide who could and who couldn't take part in these social media. 'It is very important to have a coordinated approach because you don't want your customers to have a confusing experience online with your brand,' says Sheldon. The first thing the company did was to put a central team and a central policy in place, so that people understood there were things they just couldn't mention outside the company regardless of the medium. 'Profits, for example. That we have a social media policy in place that I think is for kind of two reasons really. Firstly, it's to protect our brand online and secondly it's to protect our people, to help our people understand the implications of what they're saying and what they're doing,' says Sheldon.

It's worth clarifying at this stage that Sage is a publicly listed business, so offering hints about its financial performance would count as insider trading and be completely illegal. This isn't some sort of corporate clampdown, then; it's compliance with the law, and it's as simple as that.

Brand Control

If your business is going to be using social commerce and has been around for a while, one of the things you may have to do is to tidy up your branding. This is your 'digital shadow' – the reviews, the emails, the presentations you've left behind.

Yo! Sushi found that it had another related problem. When marketing head Mark McCulloch started the company's Facebook and Twitter pages he found there was already a presence online. First there was a member of the public with a Yo! Sushi branded Facebook page; he wasn't a fan, there were disparaging messages, and he had about 9000 members. Letters to Facebook enabled this page to be taken down – Yo! Sushi owned the trademarked name after all – but Facebook wouldn't transfer all of the members across to the new official page, reasonably enough, because that wasn't something they'd joined.

There was also a handful of local managers who'd put up Facebook pages or Twitter feeds with the company's name, 80 followers, and messages like 'I'm looking for a new flat, can anyone help'? This was easier to stop.

Something Sheldon is well aware of – although she doesn't use this exact term – is the idea that your digital shadow will be around for a while. This needs planning. 'You need to work out how it's going to look in a year's time, how you're going to constantly add new content to it that's going to be fresh, interesting.' she says. Which clearly means bringing more people in.

Initially there was a lot of hand holding. An experienced copywriter, Sheldon was quite used to the myth that everyone can write and will do when left to their own devices. She quickly found, predictably, that she was surrounded by people who didn't 'get' social media, who didn't understand that their daily tasks could make an interesting blog entry for someone to read, or that they actually had anything that could be turned into useful content. 'A lot of what we did was about educating them as to how, okay, now that you've done a great guide, how can we turn that into a blog post, how can we turn that into a Tweet.'

Repurposing: making your digital shadow work harder

In this chapter I establish that your digital shadow casts quite a long image in front of you. It means people come to you with certain expectations of certain behaviours because they have seen them in the past.

Cath Sheldon's experience at Sage, however, suggests that this can be turned to your advantage. Content can be 'repurposed' – or re-used as I prefer to think of it in English. Consider the following example:

- Salesperson makes a substantial sale, company profit is immediately improved.
- With the approval of the client this can be written up as a press release.
- This can be re-used with tweaks as a case study on your site, after the press has finished with it.
- Linking from this to Facebook can spark discussions if there were any interesting features in the sale.
- Linking again from your Twitter stream or LinkedIn will add not only to the number of people looking and hopefully taking part, but will also offer another incoming link and so boost SEO.
- Is there scope for turning the case study into video . . . ?

Of course there is the danger of overkill. By the time they've seen it on your site, Facebook, Twitter, and Vimeo some of your clients will be sick of hearing of the case study in question. And your client in the case study might by now be finding you a little on the insistent side when it comes to drawing attention to them (and heaven forbid there's a problem for everyone to retweet).

But as an idea, re-using content makes sense if done judiciously.

Measuring the effect and gaining influence

All of which means not a great deal if there's no way to measure how effective this marketing communication and brand extension has actually been. It's worth stressing here that this chapter is about marketing communications and mind share rather than straight sales copy; although everything a business does is going to have to feed into the bottom line eventually, sales may not always be the initial objective.

There are ways of measuring influence in isolation, as it were, and there are many free or inexpensive tools to see how influential you are becoming. Here is a selection of some of the free things I've looked at in the research for this book and the last.

Google Analytics

Google Analytics is, as you'll have gathered, a measuring tool from Google. It's a piece of code that you or your developer cut and paste onto your website. The customer doesn't see it, but it generates reports you can see on the Google Analytics site itself. It tells you where they've come from (so you'll know if your Twitter feed, Google itself, your Facebook page, or something else entirely is getting you the most traffic). It tells you where they go next – so if they go off to a competitor, for example, you know you need to sharpen your sales message or put more links in to other areas on your own site.

Of course it also tells you how many people are coming to the page on which you've put it, from which you can work out what proportion become customers.

Tweetdeck, Hootsuite, Twhirl etc.

Yes, I know, these aren't strictly measuring tools. They are online or offline apps for uploading and downloading social media updates, and they work very well in that way. The thing is, you can also do a search on them for your company name. This way you have a live feed of what people are saying about your brand coming in the whole time.

How easy this is to set up will depend on the stage in your business at which you are reading this book. Mechanically it's very easy: you set up a search column, enter your business name as the search string, and just watch – the messages will appear in real time. Easy. They will have a time on them so you'll see how often you're being talked about and what people are saying.

Unless of course your business is called 'Smith,' 'Green,' 'Jones,' 'Patel,' or something equally widespread. Author Graham Greene once wrote a novel in which the main characters were called Smith, Jones, and Green; critics said he had done a fine job of identifying with the common man, but he later admitted that his sole objective had been to avoid ambulance-chasing lawyers latching onto unusual surnames in novels and suing the authors for libel on behalf of similarly-named clients.

If your business's name is something like that then you may find tracking down specific mentions of your business a little harder.

Peerindex

Peerindex (peerindex.net) is a straightforward, free website. You go to the site and enter your Twitter name, and it gives you a score out of 100 based on a number of factors including the size of your audience, your activity levels, and the authority with which you speak. It establishes authority no doubt by the amount of people who retweet what you say. More usefully it then tells you about the areas in which you are influential.

Klout

'Everyone has Klout – discover yours!' screeches the front page of the Klout.com website. Once again it takes your Twitter user name and also it will look at your Facebook profile, apply some metrics, and even tell you who you're influencing. Perhaps more pertinently than Peerindex it tells you how many 'effective' followers you have; in other words how many of your thousands of followers are likely to pay you any attention. My figure there was about 40% which is quite high.

What it doesn't do – and neither can Peerindex or any other 'vanilla' influence scoring systems like these – is to put this into any sort of context.

I'll give you an example. Peerindex tells you about the stuff on which you're influential, as does Klout. One of these measurement sites says I'm influential about social media, technology, business – as you might hope if you'd been an author of a social media book previously. Peerindex says I'm influential about suits.

Suits. Things you wear. OK, I have a men's style blog, LifeOver35.com, and I do write about suits occasionally. On the blog there is a click-through to a tailor who offers loyalty points. Tracking this I can see that 24 people have made appointments through the site – this is worldwide, mind – and four people have bought suits. That's my 'influence' – discuss . . .

Four people. I hope they're enjoying their suits, I wish them all the best, but if I worked in the menswear department of a shop I'd consider influencing four people in a year to buy a suit a completely pathetic result. Anyone who's met me will know just how convincing a fashion icon I make – but the metrics this site applies, including the amount of times I mention a subject, the number of people who retweet it, and so forth, suggest I'm influential in that area.

The reason is simple – none of these sites ever gets a proper question asked of them. 'How influential am I?' doesn't mean anything until you've established who you want to influence and what you'd like them to do. There are thousands of possibilities; make new friends, gain more consultancy, sell more products or services, find a service – those are just the obvious ones. 'Influence' would mean a different thing when measured by each of these criteria.

Which is why, on balance, I still think there is only one effective measure of social media impact. Are you making more profit – is your time making you more money than it was before you started?

That's what would matter to me. If you're still inclined to use other tools to measure, let's assume they'll be different by the time this book comes out compared to what they are while I'm writing. Try to make sure of the following:

- They bear some relation to the task you're trying to achieve

- They take account of more than one social network – the Twitter-only ones are too inflexible

- They break down your 'influence' into meaningful chunks

- Above all, they don't compulsorily Tweet or Facebook your influence so everyone can see you've been checking up on yourself. Been there, done that . . .

Bloggers and other influencers

So far we've looked at how your digital 'shadow' forms and some strategies for a proactive marketing communications programme from Sage. But what happens when the digital impressions people get are completely beyond your control?

Blogging is still very important to the digital world. Engaging with bloggers is very different from engaging with journalists – and I speak as someone who does both things.

First let's establish a few ground rules. When I say 'bloggers' I'm not talking about the people who do it as an extension of a full-time or freelance post in the national press or a magazine. I'm also not talking about people who are paid to blog for some of the daily news feeds which are around. I do a fair bit of that but the rules are basically the same as they are for journalists – send the press release, assume everything is on the record, and assume the writer is being paid for what they're putting onto the screen so there is definitely some sort of comeback if something goes wrong.

No, I'm talking about the independent blogger, who may carry a little advertising but probably doesn't. I've had some experiences with some of them which it may be instructive to share.

Getting information to them

The first thing you need to understand about the smaller (but possibly very influential) blogger is that he or she may not perceive themselves as a journalist. This can mean they'll see themselves operating outside the usual means of getting information around. I'll give you an example; just too late for inclusion in my first book, a blogger put a note on his Twitter feed asking PR people not to clog up his email with press releases.

His Twitter profile said he was a blogger and information junkie. I took this up with him and he informed me, firmly, that since he hadn't put a note on his profile saying 'please send press releases to my work account' it was quite reasonable for him to object when people did so.

I still don't agree; you describe yourself as wanting information and offer to publish – people will respond. There is really no point in complaining – but this is an attitude endemic among some bloggers. They don't see themselves as part of the press machine and will resist the standard press entreaties.

They also don't expect to get paid for their work so there is arguably less comeback when you feel an opinion is unfair or that there has been some sort of misrepresentation. A journalist, for example, should never write about you or your company without at least trying to get in touch so you can put your side of the story, unless they are offering a strict commentary on already established facts, the 'opinion piece' style of journalism. Bloggers are a lot like the personality columns in the newspapers so they may or may not engage with you before writing.

(Of course a lot will depend on what you actually do – if someone is a blogger reviewing a product it might not be appropriate for them to consult with the company that made it first.)

Ways of engaging

Once you've identified a blog with which you'd like to make contact it's worth being a little careful. Experience shows that some – not all – will react badly to an approach from someone who is avowedly and respectably a PR or marketing person. So, select the person to make the approach carefully.

It's worth starting by commenting on the blog itself, without at any stage being pushy or too corporate. As with any social media, go out of your way to make yourself a useful member of the community and you're likely to end up more trusted than others. As to what to do after the connection has been established, it's a matter of learning what the blogger wants or doesn't – see the box for things that have worked and things that have failed, and given the disparate bunch bloggers actually are, don't be surprised at the contradictions!

Stuff that's worked, stuff that hasn't

Lunches: A colleague of mine was on a social media course in 2010 and the expert tutor said bloggers were usually amateurs who didn't pay themselves, so they were grateful to be taken out to lunch occasionally. Journalists, he said, were likely either not to have time or to take a lavish lunch in their stride.

He was right about the journalists' view. Personally I think I'd find his thoughts on bloggers hopelessly patronizing – little lambs need feeding up, do they, don't get out much, do they? Look, by all means suggest treating a blogger to lunch, but expect them to have as many penetrating questions as the best journalists if they're any good. And don't expect them to be amateurs working in their spare rooms – many of them are, many of them aren't.

Free goods: In journalism as well as in blogging there is a debate among public relations executives as to whether it's a good idea to ask for review samples back. My own view is simple: if someone sends me something to review it is their property. I will make it clear at the outset that they'll need to arrange return delivery charges but it's not mine to keep. Sometimes the economics mean it's not worth getting back and sometimes – take the men's aftershave/colognes I review on my LifeOver35 blog – it would be absurd to ask for it back as nobody really wants a part-used bottle of smellies. Watch out for the hoarder who is just after free gifts – by all means send a few along but do check how many readers he or she is actually getting. Unless you want to send me some aftershave or a Rolex.

There are bloggers who will assume a review sample is a gift unless someone says something to the contrary at the outset. There are bloggers (and journalists!) who set themselves a task of scrounging as many decent freebies as they can. There are others who will sense they are being bribed.

Finally on bloggers, don't be put off by the flannel that has appeared in the press about how bloggers are sad individuals hunched over their computers in damp cellars (a senior UK journalist actually said something like that in 2011). This is frequently written by journalists who are terrified of the effect blogging is having on their industry; to the reader the words are a lot more important than any prejudice against the reader.

Communicating with different audiences

In this chapter I've examined the digital 'shadow' a business and individual casts. I've had a look at the proactive stuff that's within your control and being aware of the stuff other people will generate around you, and how, in a larger organization, it's important to look at who is handling your social media and for what purpose.

I've also had a look at blogging and the expectations of the bloggers themselves – although I do stress there are no fixed rules or opinions shared by all bloggers.

Action points

- Do an audit of your digital footprint so far. Look for blogs, reviews, Tweets, mentions on other social media. If you've presented to an audience see if you can find out whether any of them mentioned you on a social network, reviewed you on a blog – find out the extent to which your reputation is already being formed through the digital channels.

- If there is any perception you feel needs addressing out there already, don't be in too much of a hurry to tackle it. Reflect and preferably evolve a strategy – do you respond to bad reviews, and if so to what end? You're not going to change the reviewer's mind.

- Consider any content you have – manuals, newsletters, anything – that can be re-purposed and turned into social content.

- Check the tools suggested for evaluating your online influence, but bear in mind that 'influence' actually has to mean something.

- Find out which blogs your customers read and read them yourself. Engage with the bloggers if it is appropriate.

9 SHOW ME THE MONEY – MEASURING ROI

n both this book and my last book *This is Social Media*, I've been keen to stress that regardless of what the various hypesters and marketeers will tell you, social media interaction isn't free. One of my favourite tricks at social media seminars is to kick off by asking how much it costs to put a YouTube video online. The answer, usually, is 'nothing.' My response is that this is perfectly correct as long as you value your time, or that of the person doing the upload, at zero as I've said elsewhere. Immediately you start paying them, or paying someone to demonstrate the upload for the first time so you're paying two people, the costs start mounting up.

Of course the costs are tiny if you're just doing the one upload but then nobody with any sense is going to leave it at a single upload. You're going to be talking about paying people to interact, to sit and put entries onto Facebook pages, and to send answers to queries.

This all needs to be costed and the desired outcome from your social media engagement will need to make this cost worthwhile. That much is self-evident. In this chapter we will be more interested in the 'deliberate' freebies – the stuff you give away for nothing whilst knowing precisely what you're doing. There is a calculation in here and it's a little different on social media from how it is elsewhere in the bricks and mortar world. Many people use their social media engagement to offer free goods and services and many succeed very well in doing so.

Free promotions can work in a number of contexts. That's what this chapter's about. You should find out about:

● Making your freebie tailored and relevant

● Making it part of your overall digital strategy

● Turning the freebie into a gateway

● Valuing the time you spend on customer engagement without payment

● Turning the freebie into something of value.

Hey you, want a free iPad?

OK, that was a trick heading. If you're reading this book in sequential order rather than dipping in – which is of course also fine – then you've seen a variant of that sentence before as an introduction to a chapter.

It's only one repetition but it's probably starting to grate already. Why, you ask, is Capstone paying this author who can't even fill 50,000 words with original thoughts – what is the point? Many people would have some sympathy with that view. Now magnify it so that not only have you seen the sentence twice in the same book but you've seen it twice in an hour – call it five times a day on your Twitter stream. It's really annoying now, isn't it – and it can't, just can't, be from companies which all have an interest in iPads as part of their business. So not only is it something you could reasonably describe as 'spam,' it's irrelevant spam to you and to the sender.

In the chapter on finding new business we discussed how to tailor offerings a little. To recap, every freebie you offer really needs to be:

● Relevant to your business

● Relevant to your target customer.

Nobody has written down any formal rules as such but if you follow the two above and assume that 'they'll like to win something' isn't good enough to qualify as 'relevant to the customer' you'll have made a bit of a start.

Just enough cooks

One way of making sure your free offering doesn't end up damaging your business is to make it so cheap you'd have to be a genius to lose much out of it even if you don't get any sales at all. Jo Maloney is head of two businesses, The Cupcake Sanctuary and

Biccies.com. She certainly doesn't lose out through her giveaways but since the retail prices are inexpensive and the trade price is accordingly even lower she'd have to hand deliver them all by helicopter to lose a great deal.

'We make gourmet cup cakes for corporate events, for birthdays, anniversaries, weddings, that kind of thing,' she says. 'We found that when we were working from home the best way to get all of our information out about what we were doing was through the social networking sites.' There were two reasons for this. First advertising through traditional newspapers and magazines was beyond this particular start-up's budget; reaching the right people whilst not committing financial suicide was important so the business went to Twitter and Facebook instead.

This is an important point to note. Throughout this book and most of the last one, I wrote as though people had a choice of which media they worked through. Budgetary considerations mean some businesses may not, so producing the right amount of people on a social networking site may be the best alternative available to them.

Armed with this need to produce publicity for negligible costs the next thing was to find a way of building up social media numbers. This was where the companies' first socially distributed giveaways came into play. Quite simply The Cupcake Sanctuary asked people to recruit their friends as members of the Facebook page and whoever got the most followers received something cupcake-related.

People reacted well and it was obvious from interactions that the people who had logged on had an interest in cupcakes – there were a lot of amateur bakers, for example. So Maloney set about tailoring the next competition to their interests. 'I set a competition based around flavours. People suggested flavours for cupcakes and when someone actually wins we send them a box of cupcakes they've effectively designed.' The interest keeps the vibe going, she explains; the business has a bit of a reputation for unusual flavours in its cakes so there is no problem with centring competitions around that theme.

Competitions like this have side benefits as well. If enough people are nominating a particular flavour then it becomes clear there is a market for it. Maloney is happy to consider including a popular new flavour into the regular offerings if that's what the market wants and thanks to giving a few items away she gets almost instant feedback at a remarkably low cost (just that of her time and a few giveaways at cost price).

The business lends itself to themed giveaways of course, and this is something of which it takes full advantage. Wedding cakes – nominating a friend for a free wedding cake or telling the business why you should have your own wedding cake for free are both ideas which have gone down well in the past. 'Out of that, we usually get around four or five orders back,' she says. 'That's a minimum order of £150 for a wedding cake so it becomes much more economical for us to carry on doing it.'

There is in fact a simple equation you can apply to a promotion in this way:

$$\text{Income from promotion} - \text{cost of promotion} = \text{a profitable figure}$$

. . . if that equation doesn't hold good then clearly the promotion has failed. Cakes at cost price, even a wedding cake, remains a lower overhead than a newspaper promotion.

Another feature of 'social' that benefits the business is the immediacy of it. 'If tomorrow is a big baking day I can put a notice up saying we're going to have a certain product on offer, come and pick it up today and you can have £5 off, then it's usually gone within 20 minutes,' says Maloney. This isn't because the company has made too many, for example, but because it always plans for a surplus in case something ends up looking not quite right. If someone has a birthday then it makes a great alternative. 'If you'd put something in a newspaper like a voucher, you're looking at a deadline of a month before you reap the benefit.' Remarkably the company hasn't had any no-shows as yet – people say they'll be there and they arrive.

The Cupcake Sanctuary

Restaurant/Café · Chatham, Medway

Wall   The Cupcake Sanctuary · **Everyone (Most Recent)** ▼

The Cupcake Sanctuary
Suchards chocolate, Mint, Winter Spice, Cinnamon and Tiramisu and thats just the flavours of Hot Chocolate we have in store. Boy it is nippy out there today

about an hour ago

👍 2 people like this.

The Cupcake Sanctuary
wow what day just had a call from a events company and they have just ordered 30 carved pumpkins. god my hands will be sore

Order your Carved Halloween Pumpkins
by: The Cupcake Sanctuary
Photos: **27**

Share · Yesterday at 11:36

👍 8 people like this.

Yesterday at 12:45

The Cupcake Sanctuary that means so much. I wont say it is easy far from it. i am working 8 days a week, I hardly get to see my kids (at the moment). But i am doing something i love. I have a fantastic husband and amazing team. As i see it if i drive the business to were i want it to be then i can give my husband and kids everything they need.
Yesterday at 13:01

Biccies

The more recent business, Biccies.com, is newer and operates more nationally than locally. It ramped up its Facebook page very quickly and once again encouraged people to join with free offers – nothing sophisticated, just picking random people to receive gifts. They almost always put a review up on the Facebook page, which again prompts a debate on the sort of biscuit box the customer would like to see in the Biccies range. 'It's just the most affordable way of hitting so many people in one go.' Of course the feedback forms free marketing information and helps with product development. 'Someone could come up with something we haven't thought of and it's always an option to put it in,' she says. 'We'd then send the suggester a box that they'd effectively designed, so it becomes a very interactive page rather than just something to tell people what's going on.'

Maloney stresses that the business doesn't expect everything for free. It has been involved in paid-for promotions and social is one element of the mix of things that have worked for the business. By assessing the likely participants and the outcomes both businesses have grown very nicely through giving things away – other businesses applying the same sort of rigour should do the same.

The disguised freebie – discounting for more business

There are perfectly standard giveaways that many companies offer, on their websites, online, and through other means. There is nothing new about a promotion as long as someone has sat down and thought it through.

There are, though, other means of reducing inventory through social media, or catering for quiet days when a service centre is empty. Jo Maloney controls her stock of cakes very carefully and is well aware of how many are likely to sell. She therefore doesn't end up with cakes near their sell-by date. Supermarkets do and they almost always have a 'reduced' shelf on which to clear their soon-to-expire wares.

There are ways of getting around this problem using social media. Suppose, for example, you had a cake company yourself and you'd overestimated the amount of product that was going to sell on a Monday. If your customers are connected most of the time then how about dropping them a note on Twitter or Facebook: '30% off cakes for the next hour, come in and mention Twitter' or something similar. If you have local people online you should find some of them will turn up, and 30% off might not be massively profitable but it's better than throwing stock away.

It works in service industries as well. Hair salons are notoriously quiet on Tuesdays, an old barber of mine once told me. They would often have fewer people on as a result and the business could still be pretty dead. Unless, of course, they Tweet out that there's a promotion on for the rest of the day for Twitter followers only. The followers will be delighted by the apparent bargain and if it's really about getting footfall that's fine, they're not naïve, they know what January sales and other promotions are about.

To scrounge is human

Early on in this book I mentioned that people were accustomed to getting stuff for free on the Internet. It's getting more and more to be the norm. Humans are very much like dogs in a way; we're creatures of habit and if you get us used to the idea that things will be free then it's very difficult to turn that around into the expectation that things will need to be paid for instead. In the 'Diving In' chapter we touched on customers accustomed to a massive discount being uninterested in coming back at the full price; people scouring the Internet for freebies are likewise not all going to come back with cash in their hand.

Indeed, there are people whose sole aim on the Internet – or in magazines, or any other medium in which there are free things to be had – is to go and help themselves to everything they possibly can. That's not a criticism: if someone is handing free stuff out, why not? In commercial terms these are people to avoid, of course, because they won't spend any money with you. One good way to handle this is to make the prizes of a low enough value so that it doesn't matter if a particular attempt is wasted – remember earlier in the book the guys from Bulldog gave away under a fiver's worth of moisturiser but it didn't matter because people were having fun with it? The other is to make sure any prize you give away is so targeted that only the relevant audience is going to be remotely interested, as happened in one of the case studies in this chapter.

The solicitor will see you now

Giving examples of your work away is frankly quite easy if your product is something like biscuits or cakes. Everybody likes a free box of biscuits. But what if your business doesn't have something as appealing to give away?

Take law firms for example. Eversheds is in a different position. Free lawsuits are never going to be a vote winner, in fact even as I type it the idea seems on the distasteful side of ludicrous. Believe it or not though, law firm Eversheds found a way of using social media for useful interactions and even a form of freebie in a contest designed for people who wanted to get to know the company a bit better with a view to working there.

Trainee solicitor Ismat Abidi was behind the competition. The concept was simple: get the company and its recruitment programme onto Twitter and Facebook where most of the candidates for coming and working with Eversheds were spending time online and offer them coffee – that's coffee with a trainee at the firm and another prize of a coffee with a partner so that they can really get a feel for the place.

Abidi, working strictly in conjunction with the human resources and the communications department within the firm, started engaging potential candidates on a Twitter account she called Legaltrainee as well as a presence on Facebook and a new social media platform called Brave New Talent for a couple of months before starting to promote the prize. She recommended early on that any competition should have more going for it than a commodity gadget style offering for the winner. 'You do get engagement through those things and they are fun, but given the current climate it wouldn't provide an experience – which is difficult to get at the moment.'

There was a lot of discussion with the trainees and the firm realized that what people really wanted was the proverbial foot in the door – and that a social media account was the perfect means through which this could be offered. This, the firm believes, is the first time anything like this has been offered as a prize by a professional service company.

A couple of points stand out immediately. First, although this may be the first such prize on offer there's no copyright on ideas so it can be mimicked. Second, it was tailored around exact feedback from the student population who'd be taking part. 'We can guarantee that the entries come from people who are interested in the firm and who genuinely want that experience,' says Abidi, reasonably enough. A prize this specific naturally leads people to self-select for appropriacy.

The way it worked was that the competition was mentioned on each of the platforms but it actually took place on Twitter. This ensured the engagement went to the place the firm actually wanted. Terms and conditions were freely available on the website and throughout the networks.

The format was that winners were selected at random from the first 500 Twitter followers and the same at 1000. Service companies looking for ideas might like to consider this quite seriously; there was no simple repetition of a marketing message, only genuine interaction from interested people. It wasn't quite as basic as that; there were criteria about whether someone had applied for a training contract and whether they were a recent graduate. To signal their compliance they were asked to put the @legaltrainee name into their Twitter profile.

Again, this is a shrewd move. One legal trainee will inevitably know another and will check their Twitter account, find the @legaltrainee account mentioned and have a look. Many will start to follow.

At the time of writing the promotion was only a couple of days old so it was impossible to say whether it will have had a material effect on the recruitment process. Certainly candidates will be better informed about the company they are approaching, and the early feedback was good in terms of retweets, appearances online, and follower growth – 40 joined in one evening. 'If I were a candidate now I would have jumped at the chance to take part in this,' says Abidi.

This could of course have been achieved through other means – email or the organization's own website being the obvious examples. Social media were deemed the right place. 'It was the place to address the current generation. It's becoming more popular year after year. You see a lot of commodity industries using it but not so much the professional services,' says Abidi. 'It's just an environment where you can encourage new ideas. I think we're in a world now where we don't go out and look for information so much, it comes to us.' The fact that it was automatically international with a high level of involvement from participants was almost a side issue.

We're onto psychology and how people are changing again, which is where this book came in. The idea of a generation expecting all of the facts and information to come to them rather than going out and looking for them would of course be a radical change for everyone to adjust to. But looking at the way in which businesses are functioning, the way journalists and bloggers are gathering their facts together, the way information is being shared, it looks like a reasonable supposition.

And this is possibly the first case of a professional service industry doing it well.

Social media as a gateway to action

Clearly in neither case was the freebie the end product of the engagement. In Maloney's case very few people would worry particularly about going and buying themselves a pack of biscuits, it's not like winning a car or something. The engagement, the competition, was an end in itself. Eversheds so clearly used the competition as a gateway for interested candidates to get in touch with the company it's almost not worth repeating. Nobody, but nobody, wants to enter a competition to win a conversation with a solicitor about working at their business unless they actually want to do the same themselves – it's fully self-evident.

Readers can learn from these examples that having an end game in mind when setting out a policy of giving away freebies is always a good idea. Think of the giveaway as a gateway and tailor it so that it encourages the target customer to walk through the door.

What if everybody wants your prize?

The Eversheds example, in which people could win coffee with insiders, is very clever except in one respect. Surely it disadvantages everyone who *doesn't* get to have that personal interaction, so you end up excluding some potentially excellent candidates? And what if someone tries to get some time with someone on their own initiative, isn't that something to be encouraged rather than put off with a 'sorry, that's actually our star prize' . . . ?

Lorraine Igoe, Eversheds' resourcing advisor for graduate recruitment, said that numbers would make this impossible but it gave a good opportunity to engage with people who would be interested in law. 'We want Eversheds to be the employer of choice so it's as much an educational tool as anything, at no cost to them of course. We feel it's a win/win situation.'

And once again this isn't social media to the exclusion of all else. The organization goes to all the trade fairs and the law schools to engage with people. One of the questions candidates are always asked at the interview stage is why they are interested in working with the particular firm they've chosen; the engagement online will help, attending workshops is better, winning the competition and getting a look inside is a little extra.

All the same it's a shame to make it so competitive, isn't it? 'Year after year not everyone can secure a work placement because of competition and numbers,' says Abidi. 'Rather than seeing this as a competition in which one in 500 win, the firm sees it as an extra opportunity for all thousand entrants.'

It's just that in the strictest terms, someone wins.

Action points

There are a lot of general learnings to take away from the very specific examples we've looked at on these pages. If you took only one thing away then it should be that every competition and every straight giveaway needs to add something to the overall interaction with the client group. Old-fashioned get-a-free-holiday-quick promotions rarely if ever work.

Sometimes they do but they still need to be marketed clearly. A skin care company in 2010 offered customers the chance to win a holiday in a spa hotel in Cornwall, for example. It was a genuine prize and the hotel had its own private cove, arguably a little piece of paradise for anyone who'd care to turn up. The connection wasn't obvious to anyone who entered until they found out that the woman who owned the skincare products in the UK was actually the owner of the hotel. Would they have been better off offering a spa session at the hotel of the winner's choice and ensuring that their own products were highlighted? It's difficult to say, you'd probably have to ask the winner how they'd have felt without their free holiday.

It's difficult to imagine, though, that they would have had many referrals of new business from it. So here are some action points:

- Take any idea you have of going and buying a 'generic' prize like an iPad and shoot it unless you're Apple and make the things.

- Look at your existing customers and ask yourself what they are going to want. Don't be put off if the prize is worth only a few quid, people really don't mind that if the competition is fun.

- Make the competition or giveaway spark some conversation. Ask – assuming the prize is from your own offerings – if people wouldn't mind reviewing it. They probably won't and you'll get a lot of good feedback from others on a Facebook page as interest grows.

- Watch the costs and don't lose money.

- Be ready for the unexpected free offer. Nobody would have thought a solicitor would get business through social media until very recently, and there has been a series of them coming into the networks and trying to look unduly trendy. Coffee with an insider and a solicitor was invaluable to the applicants, though – is there a way you can share your time and service in a way people won't have anticipated like this?

- Remember to value things other than objects. Eversheds is offering solicitors' time. This allows the entrants to self-select and it also has significant value, as anyone who has ever had to engage a solicitor will be very well aware.

- Consider the logistics. If you're promising some of your time you must be able to deliver it. If you're promising to send goods out, they must be sendable – the cake company has little interest in overseas businesses and would probably struggle if someone from Australia won one of the packs of biscuits (I have no doubt they'd be sent in good faith; whether they'd survive the journey is another thing).

- Don't be afraid to give away something which is in your interests as well as that of the winner. Information on what sort of cakes to make, ideas on what the graduate recruits are going to want – this is all vital stuff and a garrulous winner will be only too pleased to share ideas. This isn't any sort of deception – they're aware the giveaway has to have some sort of payback.

- Don't feel there has to be a competition or cheesy quiz. It can be brilliant fun when pitched right, by all means, but it can also be a distraction. Both interviewees in this chapter have done very well from choosing winners at random so they can focus the discussions on what they want people to talk about.

POSTSCRIPT

I started this book with an anecdote about how the world appeared to have changed before I started writing. People were Tweeting in a live conference, people were expecting to announce their presence at a coffee bar over the Internet. Closing the book down I see things are changing again.

I'm taking my family out for a day. We are very excited – well, two of us – because we're going to see *The Doctor Who Exhibition* at London's Olympia. *Doctor Who* is one of the top family TV programmes in the UK, surrounding a time travelling face changing hero who travels the universe righting wrongs.

There are exhibits in the foyer before you get to the main thrust of the thing, which is a sort of virtual adventure in which the audience takes part. But what's interesting is that you get invited to link into the exhibition's own WiFi network. I start to wonder what for; is BBC Worldwide so insecure that they think we're going to want to check our emails and do a bit of web surfing while we wait to be spifflicated by aliens?

But no. What it is, is an idea in which you log on to this specific network, you fire up your phone's browser and it offers you information on the exhibits as you approach them. When they first appeared on the show, lots of extra little bits and pieces like that. Then at the end of the exhibition there is the inevitable souvenir shop, and you get daily discounts if you're on the network. They pop up on your phone, they're cheaper than the prices on the shelves, and if you show the phone to the checkout staff you get the cheaper price.

Let's get the cynical stuff out of the way first: this could of course be a dirt cheap gimmick to attract the gadget-obsessed *Doctor Who* fan to go and buy some daft souvenir because he or she thinks it's a bargain when simply 'not buying' would have saved them even more money. There is also the motivation of 'put the slow moving stuff on an apparently limited offer whilst persuading people they're only getting it because they're part of some sort of elite,' which can be a means of reducing stock. I'm not a cynic – much – but I acknowledge the possibility of those motivations.

The move tells us something about the shop and the exhibition's expectations of the customers. The *Doctor Who* fan is likely to fall into one of three categories. First, the vast majority are ordinary viewers who might go to an exhibition if it's there but won't queue for a t-shirt. Second, the children, who will want their parents to buy them something. Third, and probably most interesting from the social media point of view, the later adolescent/ lifetime diehard is a demographic in his or her own right. They are likely to have a lot of the shows on DVD already, and will have bought a high definition TV.

And of course they'll have a smartphone. Or rather, enough of them will have a smartphone to make the scheme worthwhile. Someone has clearly sat down with a spreadsheet and a realistic forecast of who's going to be all technology'd up and will therefore take part.

They'll be comfortable attaching this phone to a network they don't actually know. This has implications for the branding of the company offering the network and the confidence people have in it. There had been no major reports of widespread smartphone hacking as this book went to press; if this changes then presumably that trust dynamic will alter as well.

Getting at extra information this way is going to feel natural to this sub-community. They'll be out there and able to make a commercial difference to an enterprise because they're expected to respond.

There's an argument that says we shouldn't extrapolate too much from this just yet. The *Doctor Who* fan is a peculiar beast in marketing terms; he or she is likely to spend more than average on souvenirs of this sort of visit, they will be affluent and this in itself informs the idea that they'll have a mobile device.

If this were restricted to this particular exhibition it would be a fair comment. But it's not.

It's a dominant player in the Smartphone market and this is important because of the amount of tourist apps which are coming to its phones and no others. They may well point the way forward for a whole new wave of social commerce/social media applications. There are now areas in the UK in which you don't even need an app; visit particular areas of London and your Nokia phone automatically offers you a song that was written in the area so that you can listen to something genuinely local on your headphones. This marks a clear expectation that many people will have the right phone and be comfortable with using it for applications other than simply phoning.

Of course this is just a market evolving. It's a little like a discussion we could have had 15 years or so ago, when mobile phones were transitioning between being a rich person's toy and being a mainstream gadget you'd see in just about everybody's pocket. You can now say the same about Smartphones – at least if you're targeting the affluent customer.

There is of course a side issue – for the purposes of a business book – of what happens to the other customers, the great Un-Digitalized.

This is a minor issue compared to others elsewhere. In the chapter on innovation I looked at Marriott Hotels in Mumbai and spoke about the potential employees and how they were standing outside, bewildered about what might be going on in the affluent surroundings of the extremely luxurious hotel which appeared more like a fortress to them.

This isn't a book on social history or social engineering. It's not a campaigning book, it's about businesses engaging. There are massive issues surrounding the hotel and Marriott is aware of them – by offering jobs to the people it can, it's doing something about it.

Our topic for this book is of course social commerce. There are huge gains to be made by people who can take advantage of this but as I said about social media in my previous book, this has to be part of the mix and not the whole thing. Yes of course you can get a load of people together and sell them things which they couldn't afford individually. Done electronically and in a collaborative way this is becoming known as social commerce, but as I said in Chapter 1, done without the electronic overlay it still exists and is called 'retail.'

Spread the ownership around a little and you have, with an electronic overlay, crowd-sourced your funding; in the 'real world' (not that I've ever understood why people insist on creating a divide between Cyberspace and the 'real world' – if I've handed my money over and got something in return that's real enough for me) it was called the Co-Operative movement. It's being revived by newer businesses in projects like London's 'People's Supermarket' and there will no doubt be others.

My point is that there are huge assumptions in social commerce. Assumptions about your most likely customers, their levels of engagement, and what they want out of any deal; assumptions about their willingness to become part of a business rather than just buy from it. There are massive amounts of customers out there to whom these assumptions won't apply. In my last book, I said that social media had to be part of the mix; it shouldn't dominate as it applies to only part of the possible customer base. This is even truer of social commerce. It's one facet of, rather than a substitute for, a business plan.

Using the technologies and engagement techniques highlighted here, though, you should be able to make good contact with those customers, clients, and potential part-owners who want to engage in this way. Your reach should grow and your business should increase.

Good luck!

INDEX

Index compiled by Annette Musker

also available...

tweet, blog, link and post your way to business success

in print and e-book formats

thisiscapstone.com
get more

Articles + interviews
Videos + podcasts
Books + blogs
Authors + inspiration